Asien und Afrika

Beiträge des
Zentrums für Asiatische und Afrikanische Studien (ZAAS)
der Christian-Albrechts-Universität zu Kiel

Band 14

Reinhard Stewig

Istanbul 2010:
European Capital of Culture?
World City | Global City | Mega City?

EB-Verlag

Das Zentrum für Asiatische und Afrikanische Studien (ZAAS) der Christian-Albrechts-Universität zu Kiel wurde 1981 von Heribert Busse (Orientalistik), Martin Metzger (Biblische Archäologie) und Reinhard Stewig (Geographie) gegründet.

Die Beiträge werden herausgegeben von

Lutz Berger (Turkologie) – Horst Brinkhaus (Indologie) –
Anja Pistor-Hatam (Islamwissenschaft) –
Ulrich Hübner (Religionsgeschichte des Alten Testaments
und Biblische Archäologie) – Hermann Kulke (Asiatische Geschichte) –
Josef Wiesehöfer (Alte Geschichte)

Asien und Afrika

Beiträge des
Zentrums für Asiatische und Afrikanische Studien (ZAAS)
der Christian-Albrechts-Universität zu Kiel

Band 14

Reinhard Stewig

Istanbul 2010:
European Capital of Culture?
World City | Global City | Mega City?

EB-Verlag

Bibliografische Information
der Deutschen Nationalbibliothek

Die Deutsche Nationalbibliothek verzeichnet
diese Publikation in der Deutschen
Nationalbibliografie; detaillierte
bibliografische Daten sind im Internet über

http://dnb.d-nb.de abrufbar.

Alle Rechte vorbehalten.

Dieses Buch, einschließlich aller seiner Teile,
ist urheberrechtlich geschützt. Vervielfältigungen,
Übersetzungen, Mikroverfilmungen sowie die
Einspeicherung und Verarbeitung in elektronischen
Systemen bedürfen der schriftlichen Genehmigung des Verlags.

Satz/Layout: Albrecht Simon

Copyright © EB-Verlag Dr. Brandt, Berlin 2011

ISBN: 978-3-86893-044-3

Internet: www.ebverlag.de

E-Mail: post@ebverlag.de

Druck und Bindung: buch bücher dd ag, Birkach

Printed in Germany

Table of Contents

A Introduction 7
    I.   Conditions for Awarding the Title of
        "European Capital of Culture" 7
    II. Conditions for Assessing the Specification of
        World City/Global City/Mega City 9

B Istanbul 2010: European Capital of Culture? 14
    I.   Istanbul as a European City 14
    II. Istanbul as an Asiatic City 20
    III. Istanbul as an Oriental City 23
    IV. Istanbul as a Cosmopolitan City 31
        1. Westernization 31
        2. Modernization 34
        3. Globalization 39
    V. Summary: a Single Label for Istanbul? 46

C Istanbul 2010: World City/Global City/Mega City? 48
    I.   Introductory Remarks 48
    II. Relations of Byzantium and Calchedon:
        680/660 B.C.–330 A.D. 48
    III. Constantinople 330–1453: Rise to World City Rank
        and Decline 51
        1. Rise to World City Rank: 330–7th Century 52
        2. World City Rank: 7th–11th Centuries 54
        3. Decline: 11th Century–1453 56
        4. Evaluation 58

    IV. Istanbul 1453–1920: World City Rank and Decline 58
        1. World City Rank: 1453–1683 60
        2. Decline: 1683–1920 66
        3. Evaluation 71

    V. Istanbul 1920–2010: Decline and Rise to World City Rank 72
        1. Istanbul 1920–1980: Decline 73
        2. Istanbul 1980–2010: Rise to World City Rank 75

	a Introductory Remarks	75
	b The New Economic Policy in Turkey since the 1980s	76
	c Istanbul as a Financial Centre	77
	d Social Polarization in Istanbul	81
	α Mass Housing	81
	β Gated Communities	82
	γ Gentrification	83
	e Urbanization of Istanbul Province	84
	f World City Retail Infrastructure	87
	g World City Traffic Infrastructure	89
	h Istanbul as a Manufacturing City	91
	i Istanbul as a Capital of Culture	93
	α Artistic Culture	93
	β Culture of Events	94
	γ Culture for Tourists	95
	δ Night-life Culture	96
	j Evaluation	97
D	Istanbul's Identity	99
E	Publications	101

A Introduction

A first glance at the title of the present publication may evoke the impression that two different aspects are being followed, the aspect of Capital of Culture and the aspect of World Cities. Indeed, a Capital of Culture need not be a World City, just as the opposite is true: a World City need not be a Capital of Culture.

But there is a unity of approach: the search for the identity of a city. This requires – methodically – a holistic procedure. Already at the beginning it may be stated, that this search must not necessarily result in the finding of a single label for a city, but it may very well be, that the identity of a city is present in its multi-faceted structure and appearance.

I. Conditions for Awarding the Title "European Capital of Culture" (Avrupa Kültür Başkenti; Capitale Européenne de la Culture; Kulturhauptstadt Europas)

The project of awarding European cities of culture explicitly with a title was inaugurated by the Greek actress and politician Melina Mercouri in 1985 and taken up by the European Union authorities. Since 1985 and until 1999 of the fifteen member countries of the European Union each contributed a city to the list of European cities of culture, Athens appropriately being the first. Berlin was awarded in 1988.

For nomination there was – and still is – a rotation of member countries. With the enlargement of the European Union two cities were selected each year since 2000.

It shall already be mentioned here that Istanbul's title in 2010 is the first given to a city outside the territory of the European Union. For the years 2011 and 2012 the countries allowed to make proposals have already been chosen.

A list of criteria has been set up to decide about proposals. The preparatory information to be handed-in to the European Council via respective councils of the proposing states deal with the following subjects (http://www.kultur2010.de./basics.html):
 – characterization of artistic trends and styles typical of the city
 – organization of artistic performances and promotion of cultural events
 – explanation to the European public of important historical and cultural personalities and characteristics of the city
 – specific innovative activities in the cultural realm and new ways of dialogue

- facilities of access to specific artistic creations of the city
- special cultural projects for young people
- special cultural projects with the aim of intensifying social coherence
- development of an up-graded cultural tourism balancing the interests of both tourists and the local population
- incorporation of the architectural heritage of the city's development
- promotion of the dialogue between culture in Europe and other regions of the world
- propagation of the city's contribution to the European history of arts and humanities
- promotion of cultural events of European range and attraction
- promotion of creativeness
- participation of citizens and sustainability of the application
- propagation of the application with touristic effects
- propagation of international dialogue
- accentuation of the historical heritage and lifestyle of the city.

The above list is far from providing a scientific approach for the evaluation of cities to be selected as European Capitals of Culture.

Europe and Culture are the two central notions. No attempt has been made to define the essence of Europe nor is there a fixation of the boundaries of Europe on a map.

The very wide range of what is meant by culture is left open, different levels and fields of culture are not distinguished.

Instead, artistic performances (orchestras, theatres), static art displays (museums, art galleries), festivals (film, dance, jazz), meetings and conferences (with public lectures), historical monuments, architectural highlights, sporting events, natural setting are engaged to present a city as a European City of Culture. That the presentations are European is taken for granted.

A wide general public is addressed, including the city's own population, but the list of events on show reads like a promotion for tourism. It is true, the attractiveness of a city to tourists is not a small part of its identity.

II. Conditions of Assessing the Specification of World City/Global City/Mega City

The three terms possess an ambiguous quality (BRONGER 2004). They are commonly used in everyday language and by the media without much differentiation, meaning a large city with outstanding characteristics and widespread reputation. The term World City is a vague and most diffused one. The terms Global City and Mega City are of recent coinage. With the growth of the world population and the increasing number of cities, caused by rural-urban migration in the course of the 20th century, the size of towns and cities increased unproportionally.

The phenomenon of urbanization (BÄHR 1993; BÄHR, JÜRGENS 2005, pp. 33–63) changed the structure of the world population from a rural to an urban one. In 2008 the balance was tipped in favour of urban population. At the same time the growth of large cities increased tremendously since the end of the 20th century, mostly in developing countries.

In the beginning of the 20th century three cities with more than 1 million population existed; in the beginning of the 21st century there are 360 million cities. So the sheer population size of cities initiated a new distinction of size classes.

Originally the term metropolitan city was reserved to cities with a population up to 1 million (BÄHR 1993 p. 470; BRONGER 1984, 2004). The term Mega City is now used to designate cities with more than 10 million inhabitants (BÄHR, JÜRGENS 2005, p. 31).

The term Global City is of similar young age. The connection with the term globalization is obvious. While the term Mega City refers mostly to the number of inhabitants of a city, the term Global City has as its base functional connections in many fields: commerce, finance, manufacturing, culture and others between cities and areas lying far apart, but tied together by international division of labour.

Mega Cities are distinguished due to the size classes of population, Global Cities differ according to different functions and range of influence. Both types of cities lead to a rank scale, each type on its own background of content.

The terms World City, Global City and Mega City may be used without the burden of scientific meaning in common speech, but – of course – are closely connected with scientific procedures.

In the wake of widespread urbanization during the 20th century several scientific disciplines took on the task of investigating urban settlements, with the emergence of Mega Cities also very large ones, lately.

The first urban researchers were probably geographers, joined by historians, followed by economists and sociologists, lately. The strict division of scientific disciplines resulted in restricted views of the subject, a holistic approach being far away or at least postponed.

The first German geographer to deal with the subject of World Cities seems to have been OLBRICHT (1933) (cp. BRONGER 2004, p. 145). Two aspects are astonishing in his early investigation of World Cities, written in the form of an essay; one is the realization that World Cities are not only important centres of world trade, but also of culture and science – a faint idea of a holistic approach.

The other is the historical aspect on the basis of population numbers of great cities of the past. He recognizes, that in the course of history World Cities with far reaching communications need not have been million cities.

For the year 1600 OLBRICHT (1933, p. 10) draws the line between World Cities and others at 600 000 inhabitants in Europe, respectively 1.2 million in Asia. According to this statement Venice and Naples, Paris, London, Lisbon and Amsterdam were no World Cities at the time – very much in contrast to later investigations by historians (cp. BRAUDEL 1986). However for the second century after the birth of Christ the city of Rome as the political capital of the Roman Empire, covering parts of three continents, positioned at the hub of a well developed traffic system, with 1.2 million inhabitants, is considered to have been a World City (OLBRICHT 1933, p. 11).

In 1959 the 32nd National Congress of German Geographers met in Berlin. On the occasion a Festschrift was organized by SCHULTZE (1959) dealing with World Cities. Urban geographers around the globe were invited to contribute. The following cities were presented: Berlin, Paris, Rome, Stockholm, Cape Town, Tokyo, Calcutta and Buenos Aires. It was regretted that other important World Cities could not be included because of lack of contributors (SCHULTZE 1959, p. X).

As a first attempt at a systematic presentation a number of guiding principles were suggested to the participating authors (SCHULTZE 1959, pp. XI, XII).

The essays dealt more or less with the following aspects (cp. STEWIG 1964, p. 10):
– site and situation
– general spatial relations
– far reaching traffic connections
– functional development and evolution
– multi-functionality
– range of the city's institutions
– size of population, spatial extension
– morphology of the built-up area
– urban spatial population structure
– urban traffic structure
– relations between functions and structure
    (SCHULTZE 1959, pp. XI, XII; STEWIG 1964, p. 10).

The list reflects the early stage of urban geography in Germany when morphology, development, functions and structure of urban settlements were the leading aspects (HOFMEISTER 1969).

On the whole, monographic and idiographic delineations of the selected cities were presented.

A similar procedure was used by British urban geographers when (Sir Peter) HALL published his book about World Cities in 1966, considering London, Paris, the Dutch "Randstad", the Rhein-Ruhr-agglomeration, Moscow, New York and Tokyo.

Both publications reveal a rather random collection of large cities/agglomerations that are or might be ("Randstad", Rhein-Ruhr-area) World Cities.

A new stage and level of investigation of World Cities was reached when in the 1980s the number of researches was enlarged by economists and sociologists, mostly of Anglo-American origin. They proposed new and systematic aspects, but were – of course – not in favour of holistic approaches, being prevented from this by the inherent restrictions of their disciplines.

The new scientific attitude towards World Cities/Global Cities/Mega Cities was introduced by an essay of FRIEDMANN (1986). He enumerated seven hypotheses (cp. LICHTENBERGER 1998, p. 51; GERHARD 2004, p. 5) which – he believed – explain the characteristics of World Cities:
– form and extent of a city; integration in the world economy in connection with the international division of labour and globalization
– the city's function as "basing point" in the spatial organization of production and markets
– global control function of the city exercised by several business services
– major sites for the accumulation and concentration of international capital
– world cities as points of destination of large numbers of migrants
– world cities as major manifestations of industrial capitalism and of social class polarization
– world cities as generators of social costs of immense size, exceeding fiscal capacities of a state.

Though there is mention of the social involvement of the population in World Cities, the main aspect is the economic sector of World Cities. First and foremost the global control functions are of importance in many economic fields, the existence of business headquarters, of high level business services like accounting, insurance, advertising, legal services (FRIEDMANN 1986, p. 73).

FRIEDMANN (1986, p. 74) recognizes a hierarchy of World Cities and sees differences between core, i.e. industrialized countries, and peripheral and semi-peripheral, i.e. developing countries. The hierarchy distinguished primary and secondary World Cities, New York, Los Angeles, Chicago, London, Paris and Tokyo being classed primary.

The economic functions and their range as the main criterion for acknowledging World Cities, this aspect was taken up by other economists (BEAVERSTOCK, TAYLOR, SMITH 1999) and developed into a roster of World Cities. The distribution of global service centres in accountancy, advertising, banking/finance and law were used as criteria for identifying World Cities in the GaWC Inventory (Globalization and World Cities Research Group).

Their distribution allows to establish a rank order of 55 World Cities on three levels: 10 Alpha World Cities, 10 Beta World Cities and 35 Gamma World Cities (BEAVERSTOCK, TAYLOR, SMITH 1999, p. 445), the 10 Alpha World Cities being New York, Chicago, Los Angeles; London, Paris, Frankfurt, Milan; Tokyo, Singapore, Hong Kong; the 10 Beta World Cities being San Francisco,

Sidney, Toronto, Zurich, Brussels, Madrid, Mexico City, São Paulo, Moscow, Seoul (cp. GERHARD 2004, pp. 8–9-maps).

Apart from the 55 World Cities listed strong and minimal evidence has been collected for quite a number of other possible World Cities.

The research about World Cities was still enlarged by addition of another scientific discipline: sociology. This was brought about by the publications of SASSEN (2000, 2006) (cp. GERHARD 2004, p. 6).

Her attention was devoted to demographic and social conditions of World City populations. She recognized the tremendous flow of immigrants, domestically and internationally, moving into the large cities. Of course, most of these migrants were low-income people looking for a job in the informal sector. Consequently they settled in low cost housing areas, if not slums, expanding the built-up regions of the cities.

At the same time the many new jobs in the well-paid tertiary sector attracted a business elite to such cities – thus creating social polarization. The housing areas of this elite are characterized by the coming into existence of gated communities in the inner and outer city regions and also of gentrification of former low-cost housing areas.

The research of inner city social structures is a branch of traditional urban geography.

Already OLBRICHT (1933, p. 8) had recognized that World Cities are centres of culture and science, i.e. centres of creativeness, arts and universities. This aspect opens-up a new dimension of World City research, which might be called: The Cultural Turn (GERHARD 2004, p. 6).

However, it is more an intension than an actual achievement, although preparatory publications are breaking new ground (HANNERZ 1992; SCOTT 1997; KING 1997, 2007).

The subject of culture is a very large, very differentiated and very vague realm, but is well able to help explain the identity of World Cities and their world-wide reputations.

The many ways and methods of World City research represented by the scientific disciplines of urban geography, urban history, urban economy, urban demography, urban sociology and urban cultural research contribute each their own wide spectrum of different views, but are – of course – limited by their own methods of investigation not transcending the restrictions and one-sidedness of their discipline.

It is hoped that a combination of multi-fold efforts will lead to a most wanted and accepted holistic approach to World City research in the future.

B. Istanbul 2010: European Capital of Culture (Avrupa Kültür Başkenti; Capitale Européenne de la Culture; Kulturhauptstadt Europas)?

Istanbul is – no doubt – a capital of culture, but that Istanbul is a European Capital of Culture must be doubted.

If Istanbul is not a fundamentally European city what kind of a city is it then?

Traditionally the borderline between Europe and Asia runs from the Ural Mountains through the Black Sea, the Bosphorus, the Sea of Marmara and the Dardanelles to the Agean Sea.

This would mean that a city situated on both sides of the southern entrance to the Bosphorus, such as Istanbul, covering today about 40 km on the western, Thracian side, and about 40 km on the eastern, Anatolian side, is a city on two continents.

This view, naturally, is much in use for the promotion of tourism to Istanbul.

But, of course, the eastern half of the city of Istanbul is not essentially different from the western half, though there are some special features.

In fact it is worth investigating what may be European and what may be Asiatic traits of the city.

Before turning to the problem of identity of the city of Istanbul it has to be noted that its present situation is not the only aim of investigation. Istanbul is a city with a very long history, which is – no doubt – part of its identity. It's three names, Byzantium, Constantinople, Istanbul, are an introductory proof of this (STEWIG 1964; MÜLLER-WIENER 1977).

I. Istanbul as a European City

Surely, ancient Greek and Roman culture are as much considered to have contributed to the emergence of Europe as Christianity.

When, in the 7th century B.C., in the course of the second wave of ancient Greek colonisation, two urban settlements, city-states, one on the eastern side of the southern entrance to the Bosphorus, Calchedon, a little earlier than the other, Byzantium, on the western side, were founded (MERLE 1916), their structures and functions were in line with the usual procedures of the time: the establishing of a polis, with an agora and a temple on a promontory and agriculturally used fields nearby. Commercial functions existed in connection with the grain trade from the northern shores of the Black Sea to the Greek city-states in the Agean Sea (STEWIG 1964, p. 15-map).

Greek settlers dominated the population and this situation continued after the Romans extended in the last centuries before the birth of Christ their political power in the eastern Mediterranean and around the Bosphorus (JANIN 1964, map XI; STEWIG 2006, p. 54).

The existence of frontiers of the Roman Empire in the northern Balkans and in Eastern Anatolia necessitated military connections which developed across the Bosphorus, bringing to Byzantium traffic routes as part of the Roman road system and further commercial functions, a trait not unfamiliar to European cities.

At the time the capital city of the Roman Empire was, of course, Rome. The political domination of Rome ended the historical period of more or less independent Greek city-states in the Mediterranean.

A direct land-route to Rome, the via egnatia, enhanced the traffic connections of Byzantium and its ties with the west (STEWIG 1964, p. 18-map), though long distance traffic between Rome and western Asia avoided Byzantium, crossed the Aegean Sea on a southern route via Ephesus (STEWIG 1964, p. 18-map).

In the first centuries of the new millennium Germanic tribes began their migrations from central and eastern Europe in westerly and southerly directions. It was the time when the western regions of the Roman Empire in the western Mediterranean suffered most from the attacks. It was also the time when Christianity spread in the Roman Empire and reached Byzantium.

The threats to Rome induced the Roman Emperor Constantine to choose in 330 Byzantium as the new capital city of the Roman Empire, which – when the western region succumbed to the Germanic peoples – established itself – by partition in 395 – as the East-Roman, later Byzantine Empire.

In 324 Byzantium was inaugurated as the capital city and named after its founder Constantinople (HEARSAY 1963).

With the spreading of Christianity in the eastern Mediterranean the amalgamation of state and church in the Byzantine Empire in 392 and with the opulence of Byzantine life-style the conditions were created that made Constantinople from 324 until 1453, i.e. for 1129 years – with interruptions, particularly during the Fourth Crusade (1202–1204) – a truly European Capital of Culture, the remnants of which are today the heritage of the city (DUCELLIER 1986; YERASIMOS 2000).

This is not the place for a full description of this heritage, but important aspects have to be mentioned.

As far as the Christian architecture of basilicas, churches and monasteries are concerned, systematic presentations have been published by MÜLLER-WIENER (1977, pp. 39–323) and – with grand illustrations – by YERASIMOS (2000, pp. 22–152).

The Christian architecture of the past and that which ist still existing today in Istanbaul are important aspects.

The outstanding feature is St. Sophia (Hagia Sofia, Aya Sofya) (MÜLLER-WIENER 1997, pp. 84–96) – the most representative sacral building – even today – according to size and former function as the imperial state church of the Byzantine Empire and its capital city Constantinople. It is as such a monument of Christendom in the version of Greek Orthodox religion.

This building had two forerunners, the first from 360; its present appearance dates – in a large measure – from 537. Until 1453 the building served Christian purposes. After the Turkish conquest of Constantinople in 1453 the church was changed into a mosque. This meant few internal and external modifications: four rather massive minarets were added; inside a mihrap (prayer-niche) and minbar (pulpit) were installed. The building's function as a mosque ended in 1934/35 when – by order of Atatürk – it became a museum.

For very many years scaffolding disgraced the interior, but has been – on occasion of the award of the title of European Capital of Culture to Istanbul in 2010 – removed.

One of the most notable architectural features of the building is the fact that constructionally it is a splendid combination of the longitudinal hall of earlier basilica-type parish churches and central hall places of divinity with a lofty cupola/dome 55 meters high up (SCHAEFER 1978, pp. 27–43; MÜLLER, VOGEL 1999, pp. 62–63, 270–271).

Typical are also sophisticated ways of constructional support by means of walls, buttresses, pillars, semi-domes in an impressive arrangement. There is a row of 40 openings in circular fashion at the base of the cupola which fills the interior with light and evokes an elevated feeling for visitors.

In walking distance from St. Sophia the former church of St. Irene (Hagia Eirene) (MÜLLER-WIENER 1977, pp. 112–17) marks – as much as St. Sophia – the area of the first Greek settlement on the western side of the southern entrance to the Bosphorus. "St. Irene is on a basilical plan with three naves and a cupola over the meeting place of the transepts" (BOULANGER, CASE 1961, p. 54).

The building belongs to the precinct of the Topkapı Sarayı (Seraglio Palace). This prevented its transformation into a mosque. The building which was for some time used by the Ottoman military, is since 1948 a museum (Aya Irini Kilise Müzesi) and serves for concerts and events in connection with the 2010 cultural program of the city of Istanbul. A Sacred Relics and Icons Museum is to be opened in Saint Irene.

The list of the following items, which is taken from YERASIMOS's (2000, p. 382) map about the distribution of Byzantine monuments in the old parts of the city of Istanbul, contains mosques which had once been Byzantine churches. Their outward appearance and their mode of construction are still presenting in Istanbul today European Christianity. Most of the architectural details quoted are derived from BOULANGER, CASE (1961).

- The church of SS. Sergius and Bacchus, built between 527 and 536 during the reign of Justinian I. (527–565); today: Küçük Aya Sofya Camii (MÜLLER-WIENER 1977, pp. 177–183); architecturally an "irregular quadri-lateral within which is inscribed an octagon formed of the pillars holding the cupola";
- the church of the monastery of Akataleptos, today: Kalender Camii (MÜLLER-WIENER 1977, p. 153–158); "much restored and several times altered";
- the name of the church is unknown, perhaps church of Mirelaion, the church of a monastery from the 8th century and used as a funeralplace; today: Bodrum Camii (MÜLLER-WIENER 1977, pp. 103–107);
- the church of the monastery of Constantine Lips, a courtier of the Emperor Leo the Wise; completed in 908; its construction is based on a "five nave plan"; today: Feneriisa Camii (MÜLLER-WIENER 1977, pp. 126–131);
- the name of the church is unknown; today: Kilise Camii (MÜLLER-WIENER 1977, pp. 169–171); "three small naves, the one in the centre being prolonged by a semi-circular apse";
- the church of the Saviour Pantocrator; today: Mollazeyrek Camii (MÜLLER-WIENER 1977, pp. 209–215; MÜLLER-WIENER 1982, pp. 15–28); "two churches linked together by a funerary chapel"; the three churches were part of a monastery;
- the church of St. Saviour Pantapopte; today: Eskiimaret Camii (MÜLLER-WIENER 1977, pp. 120–121); the church, built over a cistern, was once part of a monastery; "of the five probable naves of the original church, only three are now left";
- the church of St. Theodosia; today: Gül Camii (Mosque of the Roses) (MÜLLER-WIENER 1977, pp. 140–143);

- the church of St. Mary of the Mongols, also: Theotokos Muchliotissa (MÜLLER-WIENER 1977, pp. 204–205);
- the church of the Pammacaristos Virgin (Blessed Virgin); today: Fethiye Camii (MÜLLER-WIENER 1977, pp. 132–135); belonged originally to a convent of nuns; "from the outside the construction is still typically Byzantine, in spite of several alterations"; originally the church had five naves;
- the church of St. Saviour of Chora, dating from Justinian I. (527–565) times; today: Kahriye Camii (MÜLLER-WIENER 1977, pp. 159–163); construction: "single nave finishing in a semi-circular apse"; "especially remarkable on account of its mosaics and its appliqués of grey, red or green veined marble";
- the church of St. John of Studion; from 463; today: Imrahor Camii (MÜLLER-WIENER 1977, pp. 147–152); construction: "three doors into the central nave and the aisles";
- the church of St. Paul or San Domenico; today: Arap Camii (MÜLLER-WIENER 1977, pp. 79–80); in contrast to all other Byzantine churches or mosques respectively, which stand in the old parts of Istanbul between the Golden Horn, the Bosphorus, the Sea of Marmara and the Great Land Wall, this church/mosque is situated a little north of the Golden Horn, in Karaköy; the church was rebuilt in the 14th century on the spot of a former Byzantine church in Italian/Gothic style; the name Arap Camii derives from the handover to Muslim refugees from Spain after the Reconquista.

Churches, converted to mosques, but retaining their typically Byzantine outward and inward appearance and construction traits in large measure, are not the only ostentations of European Christianity in present-day Istanbul.

There are – presenting Christian themes – mosaics and frescoes, particularly in two places, St. Sophia and in the Kahriye Camii. It is worth appreciating that such images still exist – after two historical onslaughts: the iconoclasm in the Byzantine Empire of the 8th century and the dislike of Islam to render human beings in portraits.

The mosaics picture Jesus Christ and his family, his mother, Virgin Mary, and his father Joseph, the earthly and unearthly entourage of Jesus Christ, i.e. martyrs, saints, apostles, angels, attendants and – on account of the Christian faith being the state religion of the Byzantine Empire – also Emperors and their wives, being residents of Constantinople. Scenes from the bible are also depicted. The quality of the mosaics is of highest level and is in no way second to those of San Marco in Venice or Monreale in Sicily, especially those in the Kahriye Camii (GORYS 2003, p. 143).

In the Aya Sofya Museum the mosaics are to be found on the tympana over doors on the ground floor and on the walls of the gynecaeum, in the galleries of the first floor (DIRIMTEKIN).

World famous is the mosaic of Christ Enthroned (and the Emperor Leo VI. kneeling beside him) on the tympanum over the Royal Door/Imperial Gate leading from the inner narthex to the central nave.

The most beautiful mosaic – to be found on the first floor – is that of Jesus Christ, flanked by the Virgin Mary and St. John the Baptist – though part of it is destroyed. On the inside of the great dome are mosaics of winged angels, lately discovered and restored.

The Kariye Camii abounds with mosaics of excellent quality and variety of subjects. There are mosaics already in the exonarthex (outer narthex).

Only some themes are selected from BOULANGER, CASE (1961, pp. 106–108):
 – Joseph is being told of the forthcoming birth of Jesus by an angel in a dream
 – the Holy family on the way to Jerusalem
 – the birth of the Saviour
 – the return from Egypt to Galilee
 – the Temptation of Christ
 – the Feeding of the Five Thousand
 – the Healing of the Paralytic
 – Jesus and the Samaritan
 – Mary receiving bread from the Archangel Gabriel
 – the Annunciation
 – the Last Judgement
 – the Apparition of Christ to his Disciples.

The most famous is perhaps – in the centre of the cupola – the complex mosaic of the infant Jesus on the lap of the Virgin Mary surrounded by 16 saints in circular arrangement.

The images of European Christianity in present-day Istanbul, enumerated so far, are all optically perceivable. There have been fundamental, invisible impacts of Christianity originating from Constantinople – in the past – which should at least be mentioned.

The starting point is the exclamation of the Roman centurion in charge of the crucifixion of Jesus Christ: "Truly this man was the son of God" (Gospel according to St. Mark 15, 39). Consequently a major controversy started within Christianity about the nature of divinity: is Jesus Christ God or a human being, or both? What about the Trinity of Divinity? What about unified confessions and prayers? Another controversial discussion led – within European Christianity – to secessions, the establishment of two Christian churches in Europe, the Roman-Catholic and the Greek-Orthodox one, of which Constantinople became – and still is – the seat of the Greek-Orthodox Patriarchate, the spiritual centre and capital of 300 million adherents world-wide (Welt der Bibel 2009, pp. 36–41).

Of the first six Ecumenical Councils (Welt der Bibel 2009, pp. 43–45) four met in Constantinople. On the first Ecumenical Council held in Nicaea in 325, not far from Constantinople, the conviction that Christ is God was laid down. This was confirmed by the second Ecumenical Council held in Constantinople in 381; there the Holy Spirit was accepted as part of the Divine Trinity. After the third Ecumenical Council at Ephesus in 431 the fourth Ecumenical Council returned to Constantinople in 451, respectively to Calchedon on the eastern side of the southern entrance to the Bosphorus. It dogmatized that Jesus Christ is of inseparable human and divine nature. The sixth Ecumenical Council held in Constantinople in 680/681 discussed particular lines of theological conceptions (Welt der Bibel 2009, pp. 36–37).

Even today Constantinople/Istanbul is a meeting place of ecumenical importance. In November 1999 high-ranking representatives of the Catholic and the Orthodox Churches met in Istanbul, though not for fundamental discussions about theological dogmas, but for the exchange of friendliness (Frankfurter Allgemeine Zeitung, 01.12.1999).

The European heritage of Istanbul does not create a fully European Capital of Culture, but surely is the historical European component of Istanbul's identity.

II. Istanbul as an Asiatic City

It may appear a little unusual when – in connection with the problem of identity of cities – the language of the inhabitants is considered to be a constitutional aspect. This is quite in line with an holistic approach.

The case of Constantinople-Istanbul with its very long history and continuity of cityness but discontinuity of spoken and written language is an interesting example. As for the languages of the citizens of Constantinople-Istanbul there is a tremendous break in the year 1453 when Ottoman Turks conquered Constantinople.

Before – since the beginning of Byzantium and Calchedon – the language spoken and written and the official language of the Byzantine Empire was Greek, an Indo-European language. Since 1453 the language of the inhabitants of Istanbul is Turkish, derived from languages belonging to the group of Turkic, i.e. Ural-Altaic languages, which are structurally very different from Indo-European languages.

The area of origin of these languages, at the same time the area of origin of Turkish peoples, who in the course of history moved westwards in several waves, is Central Asia, around the Tienshan Mountains, the Altai Mountains and Lake Baikal.

Turkish is an agglutinating language, the grammatical relation of words are expressed not as is usual in Indo-European languages by means of conjugation and declension, but by suffixes, which may amount – completely unusual to speakers acquainted with Indo-European languages – to very long compound words. Besides, the rule of vowel harmony, i.e. vowels in the suffixes must phonetically comply with vowels in the preceding syllable, is another typical trait of Turkic languages.

Greek continued to be spoken in Istanbul after 1453, but – in the course of time – by minority groups. The expansion of the Ottoman Empire brought speakers of Indo-European, Arabic, Semitic and Turkic languages from the Balkans, Southwest Asia and Northern Africa to the city; the reduction of the Ottoman Empire resulted in refugees coming to the city, enlarging some of the minority groups and enhancing the variety of languages. The modern rural-urban migration led people of different languages from within Turkey to Istanbul, not a few Kurds speaking an Indo-European language, still increasing the motley language pattern of the city. Westernization in the past, since the 19th century, and actual globalization continued to further the multi-coloured language-diversity – not untypical of World Cities.

On their westward migrations Turkic peoples, respectively tribes, came into contact with many cultures from which they adopted several characteristics. The Oğuz Turks, one of the larger tribes on their way to the west, "embraced Islam in the late tenth century" (METZ 1996, p. 13).

This led to the intrusion of Arabic words into the "language of religion and law" (METZ 1996, p. 92). "As Persian was the language of art, refined literature and diplomacy" (METZ 1996, p. 92) many Persian words became part of the Turkish language. Istanbul, as the capital of the Ottoman Empire, was particularly the city of religion and refineness with its appropriate languages.

With the awakening of nationalism in the Ottoman Empire and in Istanbul in the 19th century language reform became a political issue (METZ 1996, p. 92) and resulted in first attempts of purification of the Turkish language by replacing words considered to be non-Turkish.

At the same time – and lasting until today – intellectual citizens of Istanbul became aware of their spatial origin. When Atatürk ordered the Turkish population to adopt family names in 1934 (GROTHUSEN 1985, p. 708), it happened and still happens that names of Central Asian regions as well as names of original Turkish tribes were used as family names of modern, intellectual people and citizens of Istanbul.

Concerning the written language in Turkey and Istanbul another fundamental break occurred – by order of Atatürk in 1934 (GROTHUSEN 1985, p. 707), a deeply effective language reform: the abolition of the Arabic alphabet and the introduction of the Latin alphabet instead. This was a contribution to diminish illiteracy, but it also severed written traditional Ottoman culture from the Turkish people. It was a means of westernization.

With the adoption of the Latin alphabet written Turkish acquired the quality of phonetic transcription, making pronunciation easier, the letters serving as phonetic symbols.

In the times of Atatürk the nationalistic ideology of the Ottoman Empire in the 19th century was taken up again. Campaigns for the purification of the Turkish language continued and were supported by a society founded in 1932, the Turkish Language Society (Türk Dil Kurumu) (METZ 1996, pp. 33–34). Many new words were created. This resulted in surprises in the Turkish vocabulary. As an example from my own experience: When I came to Turkey for the first time in 1959 the Turkish word for earthquake was zelzele, today it is deprem.

The old Ottoman ideology of the 19th century propagated by the Turkish writer Ziya Gökalp, who advocated for Pan-Turanism, the unification of Turkic peoples inside the Ottoman Empire and outside in Central Asia on the base of common language (METZ 1996, p. 27), was no longer a political issue in earnest.

Today the regular weather reports of Turkish radio and television stations for Central Asian (independent) Turkic language states, the former satellites of the Soviet Union Kazakhstan, Kyrgyzstan, Uzbekistan and Turkmenistan – Tajikistan is Persian speaking – are a faint reminder of outdated Turkish Pan-Turanism.

In the imagination of the Turkish people the admiration for the three ancient empires originating from Central Asia (PETERS 1961, pp. 13–19), expanding even to Europe, but disappearing as quickly as they came into existence, the empire of Attila in the 5th century, of Tenghis/Genghis Khan in the 13th century and that of Tamerlane in the 12th century, which caused the interregnum of Ottoman rule in Anatolia in 1402–1413 – in spite of the Ottomans being brethren of Turkic origin – is still a present remembrance.

It cannot be doubted that a variation of cultural features originally closely connected with Central Asia are today a contribution to Istanbul's identity.

III. Istanbul as an Oriental City

The term Orient is first of all referring to a region stretching through North-Africa and South-West Asia from the Atlantic Ocean to the mountain ranges of Central Asia. This is an area dominated by Islam, present in two denominations, the Sunni Muslims and the Shia Muslims.

The inhabitants of Istanbul are since 1453 in the majority Muslims, mainly Sunni Muslims, and Istanbul was – as the seat of the sultan, who was caliph – as long as the Ottoman Empire existed (until the end of the first World War) – the capital of Sunni Islam. With the influence of migrants the adherents of other denominations, amongst them Alevi – considered to be a heretical sect of Islam – are also present.

The most important place of worship of Islam is the mosque. In 1994 2360 mosques have been counted in Istanbul (SÖNMEZ 1994, p. 60). With the growth of the city since then up to roughly 12 million inhabitants the number of mosques in Istanbul may today not be far away from 3000.

There is a great variety of mosques, several types can be discerned.

There is the mescit, a kind of chapel, i.e. without a mimber/minber, a pulpit, for the hatip holding a sermon, but with a mihrab/mihrap, a prayer-niche, to indicate for prayers the direction of Mecca. The mescit is often without a minaret.

There is a big range of mosques: from simplicity to opulence, from one to six minarets, from mahalle-mosque to city-mosque. Most of the mosques in Istanbul serve the people in the surrounding areas.

The mahalle-mosques are usually one-room-buildings, with a mihrap and a mimber and carpets on the floor, with a minaret and a water supply on one of the outside walls for ritual ablutions. The unsophisticated constructions are of no architectural or historical importance and no interest for tourists.

A completely contrasting type is what has been called "mosque-complex", in Turkish: külliye (GOODWIN 1971). In the centre of the külliye is a mosque, mostly an architecturally or historically distinguished one. There are a number of buildings with different functions, but all are related to the mosque:
– a medrese, a school for teaching orthodox (Sunni) law
– an imaret, a soup kitchen for the support of poor people
– perhaps a darüşşifa, a hospital
– perhaps a darülhadis, a school for advanced studies of religious law
– perhaps a dershane, a lecture hall
– definitely a şadirvan, a fountain, for ritual ablutions before prayer
– probably a türbe, a tomb or mausoleum of the mostly high-ranking founder of the mosque-complex; perhaps even several türbes for the high-ranking relatives of the founder
– perhaps a mekteb, a Koran school for young boys
– perhaps a hamam, a bath-house for warm baths, in most cases a little away from the külliye
(GOODWIN 1971, glossary, pp. 458–459).

There are not a few mosque-complexes in the old quarters of the city of Istanbul. The sometimes numerous additional buildings are proof that not only worship and religious instruction are being administered in the mosque-complexes, but that they are also charitable institutions for social purposes, for learning, for health-care, for nutritive service to the poor – typical of traditional Oriental conditions in cities before the coming of industrial society.

The most admirable mosques and mosque-complexes above the level of mahalle-mosques have been listed by GOODWIN 1971, on many pages throughout his book dealing with Ottoman architecture at large, by MÜLLER-WIENER 1977, pp. 368–491, by YERASIMOS 2000, pp. 213–377, by GORYS 2003 on many pages of her guide to the city of Istanbul.

The first examples on the following list are the top mosques and mosque-complexes of the city of Istanbul, the rest deserve slightly lesser evaluations, in descending order:
– the Sultan Ahmet-complex, also called Blue Mosque, because of the blue-green tiles on the inside walls (GOODWIN 1971, pp. 343–349; MÜLLER-WIENER 1977, pp. 470–477; GORYS 2003, pp. 94–96); the mosque, with six minarets, dates from the time of Sultan Ahmet (1603–1617); it is the most famous mosque of Istanbul, the main city mosque, intentionally juxtaposed opposite the Aya Sofya/St. Sophia; the central cupola, reaching 43 m up, is a little

lower than that of St. Sophia, but the mosque shows off with an impressive spaciousness inside; the architecture of the mosque with its sophisticated arrangement of domes and semi-domes is a hint to Byzantine influences; in the past, pilgrimages to Mecca started from the mosque; when the six minarets had been built, Sultan Ahmet felt obliged to spend a seventh minaret for the Kaaba-mosque in Mecca, to make it top again; the mosque was, of course, the centre of the complex; of the additional buildings only a few exist today, a medrese and the türbes of Sultan Ahmet and his relatives.

- the Suleymaniye-complex (GOODWIN 1971, pp. 215–239; MÜLLER-WIENER 1977, pp. 464–469; GORYS 2003, pp. 118–119); Süleyman I. (1520–1566) was the most successful sultan of the Ottoman Empire, therefore called The Magnificent; the mosque-complex was built by the most famous Ottoman architect, Sinan, between 1551 and 1557; it is still today an excellent example of an extensive mosque-complex, though some of the additional buildings are used for different (touristic) purposes; the lay-out of the complex in a spacious rectangular fashion, parallel to the central mosque with its four minarets, is impressive; one of the additional buildings was once a muvakithane, an observatory for the fixation of the times for prayer and the beginning of Ramadan (GORYS 2003, p. 118);
- the Şehzade-complex (GOODWIN 1971, p. 207; MÜLLER-WIENER 1977, pp. 479–483; GORYS 2003, pp. 124–125); the complex was built by order of Süleyman by Sinan in condolence of the early death of his dear son Mehmet; among the several additional buildings, many of them türbes, is also a tabhane, a hospice, where – in the past – travellers could lodge free for three days (GOODWIN 1971, p. 459; MÜLLER-WIENER 1977, p. 479);
- the Fatih-complex (GOODWIN 1971, pp. 121–131, 394-395; MÜLLER-WIENER 1977, pp. 405–411; GORYS 2003, pp. 121–130); Mehmet II. (1451–1481) was the conqueror of Constantinople and for this feat called Fatih, the conqueror; in 1458 the mosque was ordered to be built by an architect named Sinan, who was not the famous architect Sinan of the 16th century; when Constantine built his city on the Bosphorus as the nea Roma the seven hills had to be instituted in Constantinople, too (STEWIG 1964, p. 21-map); after Constantinople had been taken over by the Ottomans the hills of the city naturally served as the sites for representative mosque-complexes such as that of Fatih – today dominating part of the skyline of the old city-quarters; the Fatih-complex derives some of its excelleny from the extensive and regular arrangement of medreses; it lies today in a city-quarter of strict believers in the faith of Allah;

- the Beyazıt-complex (MÜLLER-WIENER 1977, pp. 384–390; GORYS 2003, pp. 104–105) was built between 1500 and 1506 on the western side of the Great Bazaar; lying in a busy inner city area, beside a square often used for demonstrations – opposite the old gate of the university of Istanbul – there was not much room left for complex characteristics; some buildings have been turned over to modern commercial uses (public library);
- the Nuruosmaniye-complex (GOODWIN 1971, pp. 328–386; GORYS 2003, p. 111) was built in the reign of Mahmut I. (1730–1754) and Osman III. (1754–1757); the architectural style is different from the ancient mosques and mosque-complexes of the city: it was the first mosque in baroque style; hard pressed by the Great Bazaar on one side and a posh modern central business district on the other side there is not much room for a complex;
- the Yeni mosque, also Yeni Valide, without a külliye, opposite the Mısır Carşısı (Egyptian Bazaar) and opposite the Galata bridge (GOODWIN 1971, pp. 339–340, 357–358; GORYS 2003, pp. 115–117); the site of the mosque surrounded on all sides today by buzzling traffic lacks the space for additional buildings;
- there is another Yeni Valide mosque not far from the landing-stage of Üsküdar (GOODWIN 1971, p. 365; GORYS 2003, pp. 176–177); it was founded in the reign of Ahmet III. (1703–1730);
- the Eyüp-complex, outside the Great Land Wall (GORYS 2003, p. 182); Eyüp is a holy place for Muslims, because the standard-bearer of Mohammed, Abu Eyup, is supposed to have died there during the first siege of Constantinople in 668/669 by Arabs; he was buried – later – in a türbe which induced high-ranking Muslims to choose Eyüp as a funeral place; many türbes besides other additional buildings and the large cemeteries form a peculiar complex;
- the Sokullu Mehmet Paşa-complex (GOODWIN 1971, pp. 272–276; MÜLLER-WIENER 1977, pp. 460–463; GORYS 2003, pp. 99–100); the mosque was ready for service in 1571, built on the substructures of a Byzantine church; besides extensive medreses there was a dershane, a lecture hall, also a tekke, a Dervish convent; in the mosque the mimber and the mihrap contain small pieces of stone from the Kaaba (GORYS 2003, p. 100);
- the Rüstem Paşa-complex (GOODWIN 1971, pp. 250–252; MÜLLER-WIENER 1977, pp. 454–455; GORYS 2003, p. 117); at the time of Süleyman the Magnificent the famous architect Sinan was ordered to built the Rüstem Paşa-complex, not far from the Mısır Carşısı, the Egyptian Bazaar, in the business centre of the city; the Taktakale hamam in the neighbourhood may be considered as belonging to the Rüstem Paşa-complex.

The list could be continued. The following mosques and mosque-complexes – all of distinction in one way or another – shall only be mentioned:
- the Mihrimah-complex next to the Great Land Wall (GOODWIN 1971, pp. 253–255; MÜLLER-WIENER 1977, pp. 441–443; GORYS 2003, pp. 136–137);
- there is another Mihrimah-complex, also called Iskele-complex, at the landing stage of Üsküdar (GOODWIN 1971, pp. 212–214; MÜLLER-WIENER 1977, pp. 424–426; GORYS 2003, p. 175);
- the Sultan Selim-complex (GOODWIN 1971, pp. 184–187; MÜLLER-WIENER 1977, pp. 476–478); beside a Byzantine cistern (STEWIG 1998);
- the Laleli-complex (GOODWIN 1971, pp. 389–391) with a local bazaar in the basement (WIRTH 2000, vol. II, plate 125);
- the Azakapı-complex (GOODWIN 1971, p. 286; MÜLLER-WIENER 1977, pp. 378–380; GORYS 2003, pp. 146–147) on the northern side of the Golden Horn, next to the Atatürk bridge, built in 1577 by Sinan;
- the Yeraltı mosque, a subterranean mosque (GORYS 2003, p. 147) on the northern side of the Golden Horn, in Karaköy, not far from the Galata bridge; built in 1757; underneath there was a Byzantine dungeon;
- the Kılıç Ali Paşa-complex (GOODWIN 1971, p. 287; MÜLLER-WIENER 1977, pp. 430–432; GORYS 2003, p. 148) north of the Golden Horn, on the side of the Bosphorus, a work of the famous Sinan in 1580; considered to be a small copy of the Aya Sofya; a hamam belongs to the complex;
- the Nusretiye-complex (GOODWIN 1971, pp. 394–417; SUMNER-BOYD, FREELY 1972, p. 476) on the western shore of the Bosphorus; nusretiye means victory – the mosque was founded by the reform sultan Mahmut II. (1730–1754) to celebrate the victory (by liquidation) over the Janissaries, the elite but aggressive troop; built by one of the family of famous Armenian architects who favoured the Ottoman Renaissance architectural style;
- the Dolmabahçe-complex (GOODWIN 1971, p. 421; GORYS 2003, pp. 160–161); together with the Dolmabahçe clock tower and the Dolmabahçe mosque – all standing a little apart – the Dolmabahçe magnificent palace forms a spectacular complex, built by another member of the clan of Armenian architects in 1853;
- the Ortaköy-mosque (GOODWIN 1971, p. 422; GORYS 2003, p. 165) next to the landing-stage of Ortaköy, once a suburb of Istanbul; built in 1854 by an Armenian architect; a picturesque site in spite of the near-by first Bosphorus bridge;
- the Şemsi Ahmet Paşa-complex (GOODWIN 1971, p. 283; GORYS 2003, p. 177) in Üsküdar, on the Anatolian side of the Bosphorus; one of the earliest mosques in Istanbul, from 1471;

- the Selimiye-mosque (GORYS 2003, p. 180) built in the reign of Sultan Selim III. (1789–1807) in Haydarpaşa (Kadıköy) on the Anatolian side of the Bosphorus, with very tall minarets immediately at the water, near the railway station.

No doubt, mosques and mosque-complexes are optically perceivable manifestations of Islam. But religious conventions of the belief in Allah are not less important for evoking Oriental impressions.

There is the attitude of the faithful during prayers: kneeling and prostrating themselves as an expression of submission to Allah, either on the carpets of a mosque or even in the open on a prayer rug.

Five times a day the müezzin calls for prayers, originally personally from a minaret; today recorded voices are to be heard. In densely populated city regions the call for prayer may not start the same moment from several mosques of the area, so the retardation can cause a disharmonic sound.

The mosques have to be entered without shoes on. Rows of shoes outside the mosques – at prayer time – are to be seen. Diminishing honesty, which is observable in urban Islamic society in such large cities as Istanbul, has caused some of the mosques to install lockers in the prayer room for shoes to be locked away during service.

Sometimes young boys in the imaginative uniform of fake soldiers may be seen, the uniform presenting the boys as (military) men who have sustained the pain of circumcision (sünnet).

The dress code of seriously faithful women requires them to wear a çarşaf in public, a black cape and black head-scarf.

In the Ramadan, the month of fasting in Islam, a number of rituals may be observed in public. Before day-break a drummer (ramazan davulcu) wakes up the faithful to enable them to eat something before a long day's fasting; the ritual is called sahur. In the evening a cannon-shot is being fired (iftar topu) to mark the time for the evening meal (iftar) to be started; today a call from the müezzin (ezzu) often replaces the cannon-shot.

There is the three days feast of bayram (şeker bayram), the sugar festivity, at the end of the month of fasting and the four days festivity of sacrifice (kurban bayram) at the beginning of a pilgrimage to Mecca. In the past the sacrifice of an animal, a sheep, with distribution of the meat to the poor, could be watched even in urban areas.

In the next chapter Istanbul will be characterized as a cosmopolitan city. But, of course, modern developments start from what existed before and this was traditional society. So as the focus on Istanbul in this publication is not only on the present situation of the city, but also on its very long history, the conditions of traditional society cannot be neglected, though there are in a number of cases today only remnants of it – with sometimes different functions.

The spatial structure of traditional Islamic cities – religion apart – is not particularly Oriental, rather the outcome of the framework of pre-industrial society which existed elsewhere.

The seat of the sovereign in a castle or palace is the one important centre of a political capital. This was the case in Istanbul where – since early Ottoman times, from the 15th to the 19th centuries – the Seraglio Palace (Topkapı Sarayı) (GOODWIN 1971, pp. 322–329; MÜLLER-WIENER 1977, pp. 495–507; GORYS 2003, pp. 71–82) stands on the first hill, on the site of the acropolis of Byzantium, almost on the spot of the ancient palaces of the Byzantine Emperors.

But Oriental features come in with part of the structure of the large palace-precinct with gardens: there is the section called Harem, which tickles the imagination of visitors and is an immense attraction for tourists.

Beside the political centre of pre-industrial cities, especially capitals, there is the commercial centre. Again, this is typical of many traditional cities of appropriate size.

In Istanbul the bazaar was laid out in early Ottoman times, not far from the Seraglio Palace, continuing the function of the site that existed in Byzantine times.

Again it is the peculiar structure of the Great Bazaar and its surroundings (WIRTH 1974/1975; WIRTH 2000; STEWIG 2009), which justifies its classification as Oriental.

The traditional bazaar served for retail and wholesale trade, local and long distance commerce of merchants and artisans and was the forerunner of modern banks.

Still to be seen are the bedestens, two in Istanbul's bazaar, where the most valuable goods were sold and stored – with different uses today. The covered bazaar streets (kapalı çarşı) still favour in some parts open shops/stalls. The traditional combination of shopkeeper and artisan is no more, artisans have left the bazaar. But some of the old massive buildings, the hans, where the wholesale and caravan trade was managed, still exist in the surroundings of the Great Bazaar, but are unattractive for tourists and used for different purposes.

The traditional architecture still in place the bazaar is but a shadow of its former functions. However, the un-informed tourist considers it as the spectacular show-case of the Orient. But the majority of the goods on sale are for the demand and predilections of tourists. The Great Bazaar of Istanbul is today a top tourist attraction.

Beside the bazaar the typical spatial structure of retail trade outside the commercial centre of cities, in Oriental and non-Oriental societies, showed a two stepped central place hierarchy: outside the bazaar were only the small stationary mahalle-bazaars and open markets on different days of the week, which still exist today. But modern developments have changed the traditional Oriental retail trade structure of the city of Istanbul entirely (STEWIG 2009).

Another aspect of traditional Oriental urban society concerns the housing areas. Homes and street-pattern are interdependent. The traditional Turkish town- or city-house (KOMÜRCÜOĞLU 1966; GOODWIN 1977, pp. 429–457; KÜÇÜKERMAN 1992; WIRTH 2000; pp. 370–376) was a transfer of the two storey wooden house of rural areas, particularly where – as in Anatolian wooded coastal mountain ranges – wood would be used for house-building. In rural areas the ground floor served for agricultural purposes, living took place in the upper storey with separate rooms for men (selamlık) and women (haremlik). In cities the ground floor served in many cases in connection with horticultural landuse, in others as workshops for artisans.

Wood as the common building material – together with the narrowness of streets – the traditional city was a pedestrian city – the houses were prone to catching fire, destroying some city-quarters completely (SEGER, PALENCSAR 2006, p. 75; STEWIG 1964, pp. 206–207). One of the effects of modernization since the 19th century was the replacement of wooden houses by those built of stone. Today there are tendencies of restoration and excellent examples for this exist near St. Sophia.

The traditional street pattern of the old quarters of the City of Istanbul (STEWIG 1964; WIRTH 2000, vol. I, pp. 52, 346–358) relied on two structural elements: main streets and cul-de-sacs.

Traffic being provided by pedestrians, horse-men, animals of burden and simple wagons (KREISER 2001, pp. 52–53), the main streets were narrow and not very straight over long distances (STEWIG 1964, pp. 212, 214).

The family as the basic unit of Oriental society – in the past and today – relied in many ways on privacy, especially in cities. Houses around a blind alley, a cul-de-sac, fulfilled the norm (STEWIG 1966). This resulted in a street pattern characterized by many cul-de-sacs, laid out in an unplanned way, but perhaps also intensionately (WIRTH 2000, pp. 346–352). The housing areas of today's gecekondu evler (shanty towns) on the fringe of Istanbul still present examples of unplanned cul-de-sacs (STEWIG 1966, pp. 42–43). Of course, modern developments, the requirements of motor traffic, changed the street pattern of the old parts of the city of Istanbul completely (STEWIG 1964, pp. 211–215; STEWIG 2006).

It is not a surprise that the Oriental features of Istanbul – very much and closely connected with religion – play a primary role with the city's identity.

IV. Istanbul as a Cosmopolitan City

In the following text cosmopolitanism will be dealt with under three headings: westernization, modernization and globalization. These are interrelated and consecutive processes which started in Istanbul in the 18th century.

Westernization, the adoption of organisational and technical innovations, occurred in two waves, the Tanzimat-wave in the 18th century and the Atatürk-wave in the 20th century.

Modernization will here be defined in a restricted way referring to socio-demographic changes, on the basis of statistics. Because more or less reliable statistics exist in Turkey only since the beginning of Republican times – with few subjects as a start, more later – the time-span is shorter.

Globalization of the economic and social fields set in massively in Istanbul – after some earlier, occasional attempts – when a new economic policy had been introduced in Turkey in the 1980s by Turgut Özal (LEWIS 1961; SHAW, SHAW 1977; MATUZ 1990; STEWIG 2000).

1. Westernization

The territorial reduction of the Ottoman Empire after its utmost extension in the middle of the 17th century as the consequence of military and political defeats stimulated a new (political) order (Tanzimat) (DAVISON 1963), which began in the last year of the reign of Mahmut II. (1808–1839) and culminated in the reign of Abdülhamit II. (1876–1909).

It started with military and educational reform (LEWIS 1961, pp. 79–84). After British connections, the sultans turned to Prussia for military aid. Helmuth von Moltke became the most famous of Prussian officers in Ottoman service. After a naval and a military engineering school had been established in 1773 and 1793 a medical school was founded. It was the beginning of education outside the realm of religion. This development continued. The first Ottoman university (darülfünun) was founded in 1846. Foreign schools, the French Galatasaray (1867), the American Protestant Robert College (1863) settled in Istanbul.

Foreign contacts were established by the Ottoman architects of the Tanzimat, high-ranking members of the administration, with Paris, Vienna, London (LEWIS 1961, p. 87). Departments of state were organized as Ministries of the Interior, War, Pious Foundations (Evkaf) (SHAW, SHAW 1977, pp. 71–76). The Grand Vezir became Prime Minister, head of the council of ministers. The legal system began to be organized with lesser ties to religion (LEWIS 1961, pp. 107–112).

The army introduced new uniforms. As headgear the turban was exchanged for the fez in 1828. European chairs and tables came in use instead of divans and cushions (LEWIS 1961, p. 100), a post road system was opened in 1834, the telegraph adopted in 1855, railways in 1856. Istanbul became the centre of railways on both sides of the Bosphorus (LEWIS 1961, p. 94). The Deutsche Bank started the construction of the so-called Bagdad railway from Istanbul in 1888. Electricity was produced: horse-drawn trams were exchanged for electric ones; ferries on the Bosphorus became steam ferries (SHAW, SHAW 1977, pp. 226–230).

Foreign investments were engaged in introducing innovations. The first Ottoman Bank (Osmanlı Bankası) was founded in 1856. An Agricultural Bank (Ziraat Bankası) followed in 1840 (MATUZ 1990, pp. 304–307). A parliament was created and existed for a limited time (SHAW, SHAW 1977, pp. 181–189). In 1876 a constitution was drafted (SHAW, SHAW 1977, p. 174). And – under influence from abroad – the foundations of Turkish nationalism were laid (SHAW, SHAW 1977, p. 301) by Ziya Gökalp in Istanbul.

Westernization had a thorough effect on the commercial structure of the city of Istanbul. Traditionally the one and only commercial centre was the bazaar area, where all sorts of commercial activities, from retail to wholesale trade, supply and demand of goods, from local to regional and international exchange, also banking activities and artisanal work, were conducted.

This changed in the second half of the 19th century. A new centre established itself, opposite the bazaar area, on the northern side of the Golden Horn. Foreign firms and the commercial activities of minority groups in Istanbul, Greeks, Armenians, Jews, played a leading role.

Foreign banks and shipping-companies settled at the waterside of Karaköy. From there, up the hill, the famous Grande Rue de Pera (today: İstiklal Caddesi) evolved as the new linear centre (STEWIG 2009, pp. 37–46).

New types of retailing appeared in the form of shops with windows and doors – instead of open stalls as in the bazaar. And – after the models of new types of retailing in London, Paris, Berlin and Vienna – department stores were founded (TOKATLI, BOYACI 1999, pp. 82–186; TIMOR 2004, pp. 117–119).

Besides lawyers and medical men settled in the Grande Rue de Pera as much as embassies and consulates of foreign nations for representation in the capital of the Ottoman Empire.

Also members of the minority groups in Istanbul choose the Grande Rue de Pera for housing.

To eliminate for pedestrians the steep ascent from Karaköy at the coast of the Golden Horn to the Grande Rue de Pera up the hill a rack-railway tunnel was built in 1874 as one of the first underground urban communications worldwide (STEWIG 2006, p. 609).

The new type of central business district – in contrast to the Great Bazaar – was an impressive manifestation of westernization in Istanbul – as long as Istanbul – until the end of the First World War – remained a capital city. When Atatürk transferred the political centre of Turkey from Istanbul to Ankara in 1923 this meant a blow to the Grande Rue de Pera and westernization of Istanbul.

The second wave of westernization started with Atatürk, in fact, it was a cultural revolution (KIENITZ 1959). Atatürk was determined to lift Turkey on to a higher level of civilization and he managed to achieve this in a dictatorial way.

The most fundamental ingression was the creation of a secular state, the separation of religion and state (LEWIS 1961). In Islam there is no organization that might be compared with the church in Christianity.

After the last session of the Ottoman Parliament in Istanbul in 1920, a new parliament was instituted in Ankara, but in a different, not really democratic way: with a one-party system. After Atatürk had left the scene through his death in 1938, a multiple-party system was introduced in 1950.

A main task was the reform of the educational system. Had education been practised before in connection with religion, an independent secular education system, was started with systematic levels of education for the general public with primary schools (ilk okul), intermediate schools (orta okul), secondary schools (lise) and universities (KIENITZ 1959, pp. 59–70). The fight against illiteracy had begun.

The change from the traditional Arabic Ottoman alphabet to the Latin alphabet in 1928 must be seen in this connection, making it easier to write Turkish (LEWIS 1961, pp. 271, 248).

Secular education was extended to women. In 1934 women were given the right to vote in parliamentary elections (LEWIS 1961, p. 283).

Citizens were required to adopt family names in 1934 (SHAW, SHAW 1977, p. 386).

A new era began with the use of the Gregorian calender and the international time code, the weekly rest day – the Friday for prayers – transferred to Sunday (LEWIS 1961, pp. 265, 283).

The metric system replaced the old measures of weight and capacity; buildings and houses were numbered. Again, the dress code for men was changed: after the abolition of the turban for the fez in 1828, the head-gear was now the hat (LEWIS 1961, pp. 261–266).

Women had to discard the veil; polygamy was abolished. The legal system was fundamentally reformed. The şeriat laws were replaced by new secular codes: secular civil law, criminal law and commercial law were based on Swiss, Italian and German models (SHAW, SHAW 1977, p. 385).

The state took over the organization of the economy (etatism) (SHAW, SHAW 1977, pp. 388–389) – from Ankara, not from Istanbul.

Of course, with so many social innovations, most of them in contrast to the old Islamic traditions, they were not easily implemented, adopted or internalized. Particularly in rural areas things remained a long time as they were and rural-urban migrants brought their traditions to Istanbul. But a city like Istanbul, hard hit by the transfer of the function of capital to Ankara, was – before all other Turkish regions – in a position to comply with the new state ideology.

2. Modernization

As already pointed out modernization will here be restricted to demographic and social changes in the time-span from the beginning of the Turkish Republic in 1923, because more or less reliable and comparable statistics about Turkey and Istanbul exist – if at all – only from that date on. The choice of subjects depends on the availability of statistics.

The changes during the transformation of society from the level of agrarian to the level of industrial society effect several fields: population, migration, mortality, fertility, literacy, household size, employment and many others. There is a range of characteristics which differ between men and women, age groups, rural and urban areas and others.

General rules of change exist which serve as a scale of evaluation of the process of societal industrialization.

Counting only the districts with urban population within the province of Istanbul the population increased the following way in the census years (Devlet Istatistik Enstitüsü 2002, p. 42):

1927	704 825	1965	1 792 071
1935	758 488	1970	2 203 337
1940	815 638	1975	2 648 006
1945	908 050	1980	2 909 455
1950	1 002 085	1985	5 560 908
1955	1 297 372	1990	6 753 929
1960	1 506 040	2000	9 085 591

This increase, which changed the urban quality of Istanbul completely, is due in a large measure to rural-urban migration with at the same time reduced mortality and high fertility in the country and in the city.

An impression of the extent of migration may be grasped by considering the share of the city population born outside the province of Istanbul and abroad (Devlet Istatistik Enstitüsü 2002, p. 44) in %:

1935	43,1	1970	63,4
1945	50,8	1975	55,0
1955	54,3	1980	61,7
1960	56,6	1985	61,0
1965	58,9	1990	62,7
		2000	62,2

The population of Istanbul is in a high degree Anatolian born. The share of Turkish provinces and countries abroad in 1990 was the following (SÖNMEZ 1994, p. 17) in %:

Sivas	4,3	Bulgaria	1,7
Kastamonu	3,0	Samsun	1,7
Kars	2,9	Ankara	1,1
Giresun	2,8	Jugoslavia	1,1
Trabzon	2,4	Zonguldak	1,0
Ordu	2,2	Gümüşhane	0,9

Erzincan	2,0	Kayseri	0,8
Malatya	1,9	Kırklareli	0,8
Sinop	1,8	Tekirdağ	0,8
Tokat	1,8	Konya	0,8
Rize	1,8	Others	21,6
Erzurum	1,7		

This means there is a motley composition of Turkish population in Istanbul.

In SEGER, PALENCSAR (2006, p. 147) a map exists showing the distribution of the regions of origin of the in-migrants.

As far as the spatial distribution of the population and the out-born population in Istanbul is concerned there are early investigations of TÜMERTEKIN, ÖZGÜÇ (1977) and TÜMERTEKIN (1979).

The decrease of mortality, a general rule of the transformation of societies, is particularly evident in the development of infant and child mortality in Istanbul (Devlet Istatistik Enstitüsü 2002, p. 48):

Infant Mortality Rate (‰)		Child Mortality Rate (‰)	
1970	132	1970	50
1975	134	1975	51
1980	106	1980	36
1985	92	1985	29
1990	57	1990	12
2000	39	2000	6

Together with the migration to Istanbul the reduction of the two kinds of mortality contributed to the population growth of the city.

Another aspect of the transformation to industrial society is the development of literacy, with differences between men and women (Devlet Istatistik Enstitüsü 2002, p. 45) in Istanbul:

Total proportion of illiteracy (%)		Men	Women
1935	40,6	31,9	50,1
1940	36,1	28,3	45,3
1945	31,9	24,9	40,6
1950	29,4	22,5	37,2
1955	29,4	19,3	34,4
1960	26,7	19,2	36,0
1965	22,5	14,4	32,3
1970	20,6	12,6	30,0
1975	16,8	8,9	25,8
1980	16,4	9,0	24,7
1985	9,7	4,8	15,0
2000	6,6	2,8	10,5

The rate of diminishing illiteracy in Istanbul should be seen in contrast to the situation of the country as a whole (Devlet Istatistik Enstitüsü 2002, p. 65):

Total proportion of illiteracy (%)		Men	Women
1935	80,7	42,2	57,7
1940	75,4	42,2	57,7
1945	69,7	40,2	59,7
1950	67,1	40,4	59,5
1955	58,8	37,8	62,1
1960	60,4	39,0	60,9
1965	51,2	35,6	64,3
1970	43,7	34,2	65,7
1975	36,2	33,7	66,2
1980	32,5	31,1	68,8
1985	22,5	30,2	69,7
1990	19,5	28,9	71,0

The transformation to industrial society is further marked – on the country level – by a reduction of the share of people employed in the primary, agrarian economic sector and an increase in the other two economic sectors, the secondary, manufacturing, and the tertiary, service sector. Of course, in a city – especially in a very large one – the share of the primary sector is from the beginning extremely low.

For the province of Istanbul, with agriculturally used areas included, the domination of the other sectors, particularly of the service sector is obvious (Devlet Istatistik Enstitüsü 2002, p. 51) in %:

Shares of	Agriculture	Industry	Construction	Services	Unknown
1980	5,5	34,4	7,1	51,2	1,7
1985	5,2	34,8	6,6	51,9	1,5
1990	5,1	33,6	8,8	50,8	1,7
2000	8,1	32,2	6,2	53,3	0,2

Another feature of transformation to industrial society – especially marked in urban areas – is the reduction of the size of households, i.e. the number of persons in the household; for Istanbul (Devlet Istatistik Enstitüsü 2002, p. 49):

1955	4,91	1980	4,46
1960	4,79	1985	4,52
1965	4,83	1990	4,39
1970	4,69	2000	3,93
1975	4,88		

This development is an effect of the difficulties connected with housing in large cities, in spite of the reduction of the number of children: the total fertility rate decreased from 2,69 in 1980 to 1,97 in 2000 in the province of Istanbul (Devlet Istatistik Enstitüsü 2002, p. 48).

In 1994 the composition of households in Istanbul was the following (SÖNMEZ 1994, p. 16):

Size of Households in % (number of persons)

1	5,8	6	9,5
2	13,7	7	7,5
3	19,0	8	2,2
4	25,5	9	0,7
5	17,0	10+	1,6

An aspect that allows a general evaluation of the standard of living in Istanbul – as an indication of the level reached on the way to industrial society – can be based on statistics which had been collected in 1991 by Berksoy and Kongar about (household-) ownership of consumer durables in Istanbul (SÖNMEZ 1995, p. 30):

Shares in % of

Refrigerators	97,4	Colour TV	90,6
Ovens	77,8	Videos	29,8
Vacuum cleaners	15,5	Computers	5,7
Automatic washing machines	49,8	(industrial) Carpets	86,9
Washing machines	73,4	Dining room	59,4
Sewing machines	60,3	Guest room	62,7
HiFi sets	39,8	Bedroom	74,0
Recorders	66,1		

A summary of all statistics quoted reveals that in the demographic, social and economic fields the urban population of Istanbul has – on the whole – developed according to the rules observable in emerging industrial societies. So the population of Istanbul can today be fairly classified as having reached the level of industrial society (STEWIG 2000, 2004).

3. Globalization

In connection with Istanbul as a cosmopolitan city globalization is understood as up-grading – in many fields – to the typical structure of very large cities around the globe.

The pre-conditions for globalization in Turkey and in Istanbul were laid around 1980. With the third Turkish military coup in 1980 and by Turgut Özal a few years earlier, when the economic policy of the country was changed entirely (AMELUNG 1989; SCHUBERT 1996; STEWIG 2000).

In the beginnings of the Republic of Turkey, in Atatürk times, after the end of the First World War, when the economically active minority groups of the Greeks, Armenians and Jews had left the country, industrialization was – private capital lacking – taken over by the state and organized by means of state-banks (etatism). The planned economy, favouring heavy and textile industry and large plants, decided about the location – not in favour of Istanbul. Turkish industry was protected against competition from abroad; marketing relied on the home market, exports were negligible. After Atatürk, who died in 1938, the domination of the state in industry and commerce was lessened, private enterprise allowed in a limited way.

The closing of the country to international economic relations could not be maintained continuously, imports began to invade the country and to worsen the financial situation. Remedy was sought in what was called import-substitution policy, meaning that imports were reduced to semi-finished goods that could be completed for the market in Turkey. The weakening of the state's hold on choice of location of industry ushered in a more favourable situation for Istanbul.

But the real, deeply effective change of economic policy came in the 1980s, when the financial situation of the state had so worsened that the World Bank and the International Monetary Fund pressed hard for change.

The new economic policy of the country can be summarized with the targets of privatization and liberalization. This brought the opening of Turkey and Istanbul to globalization (AMELUNG 1989; SCHUBERT 1996; STEWIG 2000).

Privatization meant retreat of the state from business, particularly industry and services. Liberalization meant free exchangeability of the Turkish Lira with international currencies, promotion of exports, which strengthened considerably private textile industry and other productions of durable consumer goods. Private industrialists having free choice of location preferred Istanbul – the largest agglomeration of population in the country – for their enterprises. Foreign firms, globally operating companies, discovered Turkey as apt locations for industries, for services, for business administration, for head-offices of the Turkish branch, for organizing production and sales from Istanbul.

This brought an economic boom to the city, tremendous population growth and expansion. Necessarily the many new institutions of finance and services for business administration created a new international district, Levent, with skyscrapers, in northern Istanbul, west of the Bosphorus, north of the once famous Grande Rue de Pera, the central business district that evolved in the second half of the 19th century (SEGER, PALENCSAR 2006, pp. 138–140).

The up-grading of Istanbul since the 1980s continued in several other fields.

The new function of Istanbul as the economic capital of Turkey, the many new firms in industry and services, the expansion of the city lengthened the distance between home and work-place. The growing economic potentials of the population, the development of motor traffic, the enormous increase of the number of private cars necessitated a complete renewal of the urban communication system and the street pattern (STEWIG 2006).

The traditional cul-de-sac street pattern can hardly be discovered in Istanbul today, the grid-iron pattern being the rule (STEWIG 1964).

An inner urban system of motorways was constructed with two bridges across the Bosphorus, the first in 1973 – on occasion of the 50th anniversary of the Turkish Republic – the second in 1988, both with connections to motorways. In spite of the bridges a fleet of Bosphorus ferries criss-cross the water between the Anatolian and the Thracian sides of the city, the eastern side having caught up with the spatial expansion of the western side lately (STEWIG 2006).

Besides, an inner urban rail system is being installed with underground lines – one to the new centre in northern Istanbul – and surface lines as tramways with large cars – though more remains to be done, particularly in the eastern half of Istanbul.

Of the two international airports only one, the Atatürk Airport, a modern airport since 1954, in the western fringe of the city, has rail connections, the other airport, Sabiha Gökçen, since 2001, named after the adopted daughter of Atatürk, who was the first female pilot in Turkey, situated on the extreme eastern fringe of Istanbul, is still awaiting rail connections.

Another field where fundamental changes took place in the course of globalization was the retail structure of the city of Istanbul. Had the ancient traditional centre of the Great Bazaar already suffered from competition by the emergence of the new, modern centre, the Grande Rue de Pera, north of the Golden Horn in the second half of the 19th century, competition again increased by innovations since 1980.

The enormous population growth, the extreme expansion of the city of Istanbul on both sides of the Bosphorus, the growing distance from the major retail centres in the inner city, the increasing economic potential of the population and the model of new retail centres abroad, especially in the United States, led to the introduction of modern, American-type, mall-type shopping-centres in Istanbul, first in 1988, the "Galleria" (TIMOR 2004; STEWIG 2009). Today roughly 50 modern shopping-centres exist in Istanbul, in the western, eastern and northern axes – the directions of the expansion of the city population.

For the short time-span since 1988 two waves of shopping-centre construction can be distinguished, an early wave with relatively small shopping-centres, of which several have been forced to close because of inner city shopping-centre competition, and the latest wave of the most modern, generally larger shopping-centres with up to six floors, food court, entertainments and connections to the urban traffic system, partly even to the underground system.

The shopping-centres in the inner urban areas provide underground parking, with shopping-centres in the periphery, where space is available at reasonable prices, surface parking prevails.

Most of the shopping centres offer high-ranking goods, several international labels. The clientele is not reserved to high-income customers; middle class people are the buyers (TIMOR 2004; STEWIG 2009).

The very latest development of the retail structure of the city of Istanbul is the local combination of mall-type shopping-centre and additional institutions like hospitals and others, forming an assembly that might be called commercial külliye (STEWIG 2009). In this development Istanbul seems to be a forerunner of international developments of distinction.

The retail trade structure of the city of Istanbul is fully in line with respective structures of other very large cities in industrial societies.

The aspects of housing and social structure of the population are intimately connected in any city. Again, there was a deep incision in the last three decades of the 20th century in Istanbul.

Before the 1980s the spatial urban development of Istanbul was in a high degree determined by the influx of migrants; the flow increased from a rivulet to a raging river in the course of time (SARAN 1974).

The migrants came more or less directly from Anatolian villages, so that the term has been coined: "peasants without plows" (SUZUKI 1966) are part of the population of Istanbul. The people were comparatively poor; this is why they had to care for settlements in the city themselves: the gecekondu evler, i.e. houses, mainly huts or sheds in the beginning, built overnight, a fact that – according to an old custom – allowed them to stay. The unplanned process of settlement resulted in the emergence of cul-de-sacs (STEWIG 1966, p. 43).

It would be inappropriate to call the gecekondus slums, though there was no water, no electricity, no drainage in the beginning. But the people settled in kinship groups, together with neighbours from the same village and practised rural solidarity. The settlements were areas of adjustment to urban life.

Looking for work in Istanbul the settlers preferred nearness to industrialized locations. The upper Golden Horn – on both sides – being a region of manufacturing, the migrants built their huts on the fringe; Gaziosmanpaşa became an infamous gecekondu area. The same applies to the region of Beykoz, on the Anatolian side of the northern Bosphorus, where industrial firms had been established already in the 19th century. Zeytinburnu was another large gecekondu region just outside the Great Land Wall (STEWIG 1966; TÜMERTEKIN 1971, map 2-A; KARPAT 1976; DANIELSON, KELEŞ 1985, p. 163-map).

The complete change of settlement, the restructuring of gecekondu areas, the construction of new urban housing, came at the time of the new economic policy in Turkey, though the foundation of co-operative building societies dates back a little earlier (STEWIG 2000, pp. 250–254). Mass housing construction was widely supported by the state by means of a fund (Toplu Konut Fonu) which offered subsidized credit.

Since then the urban structure of the suburbanized periphery of Istanbul changed completely: housing towers, not a few with 15 and more floors, were constructed in great numbers. This means that optically the appearance of Istanbul's housing areas is now well in line with that of other very large cities around the globe.

As long as unplanned areas with cul-de-sacs existed the so intensely desired privacy of families was unimpinched. In the new apartment-housing blocks privacy can be maintained in a lesser degree nowadays.

The development of Istanbul, the new function of economic, commercial capital of Turkey (and regions beyond) raised the income-level of the population to middle-class standard by creating many new jobs in the tertiary, the service sector.

This, of course, was a positive pre-condition for the changes of housing in Istanbul in the last decades.

The extraordinary growth of the high-ranking commercial sector created a great number of highly-paid jobs. So a managerial class emerged in Istanbul too, the managers having their own predilections for housing: gated communities came into existence, high-quality housing with protective arrangements for the potent residents. Consequently pockets of high-ranking population are also to be found in the fringe areas of Istanbul. Besides, up-grading of housing of dilapidated inner city quarters, gentrification, also took place.

The appearance of gated communities and gentrification and the legacy of low-ranking housing accommodation are in line with typical structures of cosmopolitan, large cities around the globe.

There is at least one more field which is important in connection with cosmopolitanism of cities. This is the field of culture or civilization; the notion of culture is not very practicable in the English language. Civilization is in the first place referring to ethical and technical conditions, culture more to artistic performance.

Culture and/or civilization has much to do with Istanbul's 2010 award as (European) Capital of Culture.

Culture is connected with an excessive number of features, religion, arts, science, law, economics, behaviour, education, techniques, living (Wilhelm Dilthey 1833–1911). Also the local, national or international colour of events is mostly full of cultural evidence.

Culture is meant to be received by the public. The addressees can be the resident population and/or people coming to a cultural city. This is where tourists and tourism are joined with culture. A city has to care for the accommodation of the tourists, care for hotels, which have an effect on the spatial urban structure.

There is a distinction to be made between high and low/every day culture (STEINECKE 2007, p. 5) and this applies to the supply of culture as well as to the demand, provided by the local population of a city and/or tourists.

To begin with the tourists: according not only to different cultural predilections of tourists – from high to low culture – but also the different income levels of tourists, the hotels range from top and posh quality, mostly international hotels, to cheaper lodgings. After a slow start in the first years after the Second World War with the Hilton Hotel in 1955 the increase of international hotels in Istanbul of top quality, five or four stars, is amazing (KEYDER, ÖNCÜ 1993; STEWIG 2000, p. 262; SOMER 2005, pp. 228–259). The urban spatial structure of Istanbul affords now an area where – in northern Istanbul, north of the Golden Horn, adjacent to the Grande Rue de Pera/İstiklal Caddesi – hotels, some of them skyscraper hotels, abound. Again this is an adjustment of the city of Istanbul to international, cosmopolitan standards of very large cities around the globe.

Of the cultural tourist attractions of Istanbul the impressive Byzantine survivals of Christianity are as important as the very many historical Ottoman mosques and mosque-complexes and other historical buildings of Ottoman times, especially the Seraglio Palace (Topkapı Sarayı).

The city is also a townscape of museums with a wide range of subjects, from Modern Art – recently opened in preparation for the 2010 award – to Handicrafts and Apparel (Sadberk Hanim Müzezi), to naval and technical museums; as a combination of art and industrial archaeology a former electricity generating station is used for a modern art gallery (Santralistanbul). The city abounds in small art galleries, mainly for the resident polulation (SOMER 2005, pp. 328–332).

There is also a great number of events in Istanbul, particularly festivals, a little exaggerated due to the 2010 award as (European) Capital of Culture. The events take place regularly:
– International Mystic Music Festival
– International Jazz Festival
– International Festival of Music
– International Festival of Dance

- (Efes Pilsen) International Festival of Blues
- Festival of Alternative Music
- (Akbank) Jazz Festival
- Festival of Gypsy Music
- International Film Festival
- Gay Film Festival
- International Biennial of Visual Arts, which is esteemed to be competitive with the respective event in Venice (Frankfurter Allgemeine Zeitung, 23.9.2003)
- International Theatre Festival
    (http://www.istanbulguide.net/istguide/anglais/vivre/festivals.htm).

There is in 2010 in Istanbul on occasion of the (European) Capital of Culture award an enlarged cultural program, classified under the headings earth, air, water and fire.

Sporting events are not less important for tourism in Istanbul. There is the
- International Formula One Racing event
- International Marathon event.

For a high-ranking city with a vast tourist population and a managerial resident population the existence of an international night-life scene should not be underestimated. The old Grande Rue de Pera, north of the Golden Horn, which lost so much of its multi-faceted importance when the function of political capital was transferred after the First world War from Istanbul to Ankara, experienced a fundamental transformation/re-vitalization after the Second World War, particularly since the economic boom in Turkey after the 1980s: it became the night-life centre of Istanbul, Turkey and beyond.

Another cultural, natural and historical attraction Istanbul has to offer for international tourism is the picturesque Bosphorus sea- and landscape, running through the middle of the city (STEWIG 2006). It is not only the natural beauty, but as much its valorization, which makes it attractive: old palaces from Ottoman times (Dolmabahçe, Beylerbeyi, Küçüksu), ancient castles (Rumeli Hisarı, Anadolu Hisarı), noble summer residences (yalı), from old to modern, in large numbers, on both sides of the Bosphorus, adorn the waterway.

With these attractions Istanbul excells all other large cities around the globe.

V. Summary: a Single Label for Istanbul?

The author of the present publication has no doubts that Istanbul is a Capital of Culture, but he has doubts that Istanbul is – as the award title implies – a European Capital of Culture. Many aspects have to be taken into consideration. This is why a holistic, generalistic view has been practiced in the foregoing text.

The open question is, if a single label is necessary or desirable at all, if the previous delineations are not sufficient characteristics of the identity of the city of Istanbul.

Since times immemorial peoples and impacts reached the Bosphorus from distant lands. In the 7th century B.C. the first Greek settlers of the second wave of ancient Greek colonial expansion came from the west. Before the Romans extended their empire in the last centuries B.C. and the first centuries A.D. from the west, the intermezzo of Persian invaders in the $6^{th}/5^{th}$ centuries B.C. had started from the east.

Christianity, originally at home in eastern lands, dominated the settlements at the Bosphorus for a very long time. The Crusades, of which the fourth had a disastrous effect on Constantinople in 1204, came from the west.

Since the 11th century Turkish tribes invaded Anatolia from the east, after the Battle of Manzikert/Malazgirt in 1071, and brought with them an Oriental religion, Islam, and an Asiatic language, the Turkic language, respectively Turkish (Ottoman Turkish) with many Persian and Arabic words, which dominated the settlement at the Bosphorus and its population since 1453.

In the 19th century the shrinking the Ottoman Empire and particularly Istanbul adopted technical innovations, organisational reform of political administration and national consciousness from the west. These developments continued in the Republic of Turkey and after the forced amalgamation with traditional structures and behaviours in Atatürk's times were enlarged, covering also demographic, social and economic fields of society.

The impacts from outside, from many parts of the world, still widened through the economic, social and cultural opening of Turkey by means of the new economic policy since the 1980s in a wave of globalization.

As the meeting place of outside impacts from distant lands during the full course of history the city at the Bosphorus may well be called – and this is valid for the past and for today – a crossroads city, a carrefour city (GÜVENÇ, İŞIK 2002, p. 200).

This brings us to the question about the relation between Istanbul's important traits that have been delineated.

If the term pluralistic is used to summarize Istanbul's identity, the quality of the relationship is left open; the four traits are just seen in a juxtaposition, one beside another (W. G. LERCH in Frankfurter Allgemeine Zeitung, 17.6.2010).

At this point still another question arises: have the various traits been integrated? Is the identity of the city of Istanbul that of an integrated city? The question calls for another investigation.

A guess may be allowed: at least in some fields of culture a blending seems to have taken place (cp. R. HERMANN in Frankfurter Allgemeine Zeitung, 18.6.2010). In arts and humanities, in music and sports the East and the West, the Orient and the Occident, have integrated in Istanbul.

The blending of cultures of the East and the West is being further promoted by Istanbuls's appointment to (European) Capital of Culture. The city's extensive cultural program is fully in line with this development.

In case a single label is desired: Istanbul is a crossroads economic – over long periods in the past also political – and cultural capital with a rich culture of Byzantine churches and Ottoman mosques, a city which has attained – in contrast to several regions of Turkey – the level of industrial society.

C. Istanbul 2010: World City/Global City/Mega City?

I. Introductory Remarks

When systematic investigation of World Cities started after the Second World War, the methods employed were mostly those of monographic and idiographic delineation. This was the case with HALL's book about World Cities in 1966, SCHULTZE's collection about World Cities in 1959, on occasion of the 32. German National Geographical Congress, and of my own dealing with "Byzanz – Konstantinopel – Istanbul" in 1964.

On the other hand the actual methodical approach to World Cities of economists and sociologists, FRIEDMANN 1986, SASSEN 2006, laying great stress on the long range financial function of cities as the most important criterion for World Cityness, is no less one-sided as a scientific procedure (GERHARD 2004), leaving the field of culture and other fields out of consideration and reserving World Cityness only to top ranking positions.

A not so strict approach to World Cities, more in the direction of a holistic approach, is desirable, as was suggested by BRUNN, WILLIAMS (1983, p. 486) (cp. REBITZER 1995, p. 14) including communicational and informational services, fairs and exhibitions, conferences and conventions, investigation and research institutions and the many-faceted realms of culture.

At the same time an investigation of the relation between cities, large and smaller ones, is an urgent necessity which will lead to a rank-scale of possible World Cities. This is in line with actual World City research.

Present-day World City research is focussed on present-day World Cities. The historical perspective is – with a few exceptions (ABU-LUGHOD 1989) generally missing. But, no doubt, a deeply historical city like (Byzantium-Constantinople-) Istanbul cannot do without the historical dimension as an indispensable aspect.

II. Relations of Byzantium and Calchedon: 680/660 B.B.–330 A.D.

What is today a megalopolis on the northern coast of the Sea of Marmara, stretching across the Bosphorus for more than 80 km, started as two different settlements, one on the eastern side of the southern entrance to the Bosphorus, Calchedon, one on the western side of the southern entrance to the Bosphorus,

Byzantium, the eastern one founded a little earlier, in 680 B.C., than the western one, in 660 B.C. (MERLE 1916).

Both settlements belong to the second wave of ancient Greek colonisation in the Sea of Marmara and the Black Sea (STEWIG 1964, p. 15-map). The first wave had begun about 200 years earlier and was directed from ancient Greece to the eastern coast of the Aegean Sea (BENGTSON 1960).

It need be explained how the two separate settlements grew into one and what relation existed between them and other settlements in the near and far surroundings. At this early stage the two settlements were very far from being World Cities.

The Greek settlers of the two colonies, Byzantium and Calchedon, came from a small place, Megara, on the coast of the Greek mainland, the peninsula of Attica (MERLE 1916, p. 6).

For the early period of the two colonial outposts the question has been raised, if they were agricultural or commercial settlements. MERLE (1916, pp. 9–10) maintains that because of the strong currents of the Bosphorus in an adverse direction, from the Black Sea to the Sea of Marmara, which made shipping difficult, both, Byzantium and Calchedon, were agrarian colonies in the beginning and that it took about two centuries for commerce with the Greek Black Sea colonies to commence. KIRSTEN (1956, p. 69) believes, that because of the sites of Byzantium (and Calchedon), on promontories, with little space for agriculture, commercial activities started from the beginning.

Both settlements were politically separate places and acquired in the course of ancient history the standard structure of the Greek polis (KOLB 1984, pp. 58–140). As a protection against raids of the natives from the surrounding regions walls were built. JANIN (1964, map 2) published a map of Byzantium showing the first wall around the tip of land between the Golden Horn, the Bosphorus and the Sea of Marmara. NEWSKAJA (1955, map 2) seems to have located several temples on the promontory, as much as JANIN (1964, map 2). Surely, an agora must have existed too (KOLB 1984).

Because of the later importance of Byzantium as the capital of the Byzantine Empire, the attention of scientists was oriented to the early history of that city, while Calchedon suffered from negligence.

In the ancient Greek and Roman world both cities had some commercial importance, especially with the grain trade from the Black Sea, but were politically subordinate. During the long-time political struggle in antiquity between the leading Greek city-states of Athens in Attica and Sparta in the Peloponnesus, the advance of Persian rulers, mainly Dareios I. (550 B.C.–486 B.C.), the aggression of Macedonian kings, rulers of Rome and native peoples organizing their own political units, both cities had to endure the hegemony of outside, distant political powers.

The tribute fees Byzantium and Calchedon paid to various dominant contenders, so in the 5th century B.C., are at the same time an indication of different commercial abilities – Byzantium mostly better off – and the supremacy of far away political centres (MERLE 1916, pp. 19–20; NEWSKAJA 1955, table II).

It is impracticable to guess what numbers of population might have existed in Byzantium and Calchedon. The population of both places seems to have been rather interested in connection with the grain trade of the Black Sea and also the sale of fish, which was and still is plentiful in the Bosphorus (MERLE 1916, p. 10). A duty imposed on goods passing through the Bosphorus (MERLE 1916, p. 23) contributed to the income of the city population. Arts and humanities, in which other Greek city-states excelled, do not seem to have been an activity of Byzantium and Calchedon (MERLE 1916, p. 2).

In the period from 680 B.C., respectively 660 B.C., to 330 A.D., when Byzantium became the capital of the East Roman, later Byzantine Empire, the subordination of Byzantium and Calchedon to politically leading cities changed several times.

No population figures being available for the two cities at the entrance of the Bosphorus, the city population of the dominating powers of the Mediterranean area in antiquity – if they can be relied on – may demonstrate where the big cities were located.

About 430 B.C. Athens is supposed to have had 155 000 inhabitants, Syracuse 125 000; about 200 B.C. the centre of political power shifted to Rome with 150 000 population, contending with Carthago of the same size; about 100 A.D. the city of Rome had increased to 650 000, Alexandria as the runner-up with 400 000 (BRONGER 2004, p. 168, on the basis of CHANDLER, FOX 1974; cp. RUSSELL 1958/1961, pp. 64–66).

It was the rank promotion to capital city of a large empire that brought the unification of Byzantium and Calchedon and the change of names to Constantinople.

Before, the establishment of the Kingdom of Bithynia by natives in 264 B.C. and the expansion of the Roman Empire into Asia Minor in the centuries before and after the birth of Christ caused changes. The Kingdom of Bithynia chose Nicomedia, today Izmit, as its capital (STEWIG 1969, p. 270) and incorporated Calchedon.

Byzantium remained relatively independent until the Roman Emperor Septimius Severus (193–211 A.D.) besieged and conquered it in 196 B.C. making the city part of the Roman Empire. Septimius Severus enlarged the conquered city, built a new wall west of the old one (STEWIG 1964, p. 21-map) and added typical elements of Roman cities of the time such as a hippodrome in 203 A.D. and some palaces (KOLB 1984).

Calchedon fell into oblivion.

In 74 B.C. the Kingdom of Bithynia was made a Roman province (STEWIG 1968, p. 270). Consequently the area on both sides of the Bosphorus, the western side since 196 A.D., were part of the Roman Empire, which extended far into Anatolia/Asia Minor.

Cilicia becoming a Roman province in 102 B.C., Galatia in 25 B.C., Cappadocia in 181 A.D. The Roman Empire also extended into the Balkans, creating Roman provinces there too: Moesia in 29 B.C., Thrace in 46 A.D. and Dacia in 107 A.D. (STEWIG 1969, p. 272).

The Roman Empire having to fight adversaries on two fronts, in the east, the Euphrates front in Anatolia and the Danube front in the Balkans, a military strategy – to combine the two fronts by means of a military road across the Bosphorus – was devised.

Before, the via egnatia, the Roman road leading from Byzantium across northern Greece to the Adriatic Sea and to Rome, must have contributed to making the settlement at the southern entrance of the Bosphorus an emerging crossroads city.

However, it has to be noted that the long distance land route from western Asia to the Mediterranean crossed for a long time the Aegean Sea farther south. The Royal Road (RAMSAY 1890, 1962, pp. 27–35; STEWIG 1964, p. 18-map) ran across central Anatolia to Miletos and after its decline to Ephesos as the port city to the west. Its importance as a caravan and trade route – more than a military road – is expressed by the supposed population of Ephesos at 200 000 in 100 A.D. (BRONGER 2004, p. 168).

Had Byzantium and Calchedon mostly served local and medium range functions in the past one of the pre-conditions was now laid for the things to come: promotion to World City rank as capital of the Byzantine Empire under the name of Constantinople.

III. Constantinople 330–1435: Rise to World City Rank and Decline

When in the 1980s World City research received a new impetus from economists and sociologists a new paradigm was created to decide about criteria for

World Cities. As is appropriate in advanced industrial society modern standards of organization were chosen. The stress was laid on services of many kinds, particularly financial and related services, business administration, far reaching information technology, but also polarized social structures and large city population (FRIEDMANN 1986 and others.).

Turning to historical situations of the distant past, it is clear that such criteria cannot be used for societies on a different level, that of dominating agrarian structure. Instead far reaching political functions, the spatial dimension of states, trade and international commerce, long distance transport lanes on land and sea, exchange of artisanal productions as well as size of city population are fitting criteria for decisions about historical World City status.

Problems of sufficient and useful statistics do not merely belong to the past, but to actual situations of city research as much.

From 330 A.D., when the Roman Emperor Constantine (324–337) chose Byzantium as capital of the Roman Empire, until 1453, when the Ottomans conquered the city, i.e. for 1123 years, the combined settlement on both sides of the southern entrance to the Bosphorus was called Constantinople. When the name was changed to Istanbul in 1453 the old name continued to be used in Western Europe for a long time, mainly in connection with religion (STEWIG 1967, p. 20); Istanbul remained the seat of the Greek-Orthodox and the Armenian Patriarchates until today.

As far as the spatial dimension of the world between 330 and 1453 is concerned, it was the Mediterranean world and its adjacent lands in Asia, Europe and Africa, though far distant contacts existed – Marco Polo's travels in the 13th and 14th centuries – with Central Asia and even the Far East by way of the land route. America was only discovered in 1492. Vasco da Gama sailed round Africa and opened the sea route to India in 1498.

1. Rise to World City Rank: 330–7th Century

The rise of Constantinople to World City rank has first of all to do with fundamental political and territorial changes in the Mediterranean world in the first centuries after the birth of Christ. About 100 A.D. the Roman Empire still comprised large parts of both, the eastern and western areas of the Mediterranean Sea and its adjacent lands. In 100 A.D. Rome is supposed to have had 650 000 inhabitants as a unchallenged historical World City, only surpassed by a Chinese city (BRONGER 2004, p. 168, based on CHANDLER, FOX 1974). Even

Ephesos had about 200 000 inhabitants. Byzantium was at that time a rather unimportant city with a limited population.

The great change was caused by Germanic tribes pushing south towards the centre and western areas of the Roman Empire. When Constantine transferred the political capital from Rome to Byzantium – the crossroads function of Byzantium in a long range road system was surely an invitation – the Roman Empire, ruled from Constantinople, is supposed to have covered 100 000 km^2 (KIRSTEN, BUCHHOLZ, KÖLLMANN 1956, vol. I., p. 402) at the time of Constantine (324–337).

The new function attracted population to Constantinople and the number of inhabitants is believed to have amounted to 150 000 in the 4th century (RUSSELL 1958/1961, p. 66), Rome still being larger, but rapidly declining. In the following century the population of Constantinople is supposed to have increased to about from half a million to one million (RUSSELL 1958/1961, p. 69), rapidly surpassing Rome.

The city area of Constantinople expanded as is demonstrated by the new wall-systems, the first wall built by Constantine (324–337), the second by Theodosius II. (408–450) (STEWIG 1964, p. 21-map). The second wall is the Great Land Wall which existed not only in 1453, when it was overrun, but further in Ottoman times and is still a partly restored tourist attraction today.

The internal structure of Constantinople (HEARSAY 1963, p. 3; JANIN 1964, maps 1, 5, 7) on the way to World City rank was much influenced by the amalgamation of state and church in the Byzantine Empire with St. Sophia (Aya Sofya) as the imperial state and city cathedral and the palaces of the Byzantine Emperors as dominating buildings. The first St. Sophia – reconstructions followed – was already consecrated in 360 (YERASIMOS 2000, p. 384). Typical features and structures of a Byzantine city marked Constantinople (KIRSTEN 1958).

The alliance between state and church made Constantinople more and more – after the political abandonment of Rome – the head city of the Greek Orthodox church, independent from the Roman Catholic church and the pope. Religious sovereignty was finally achieved in 1054. Before, in the religious quarrels about the essence of God, Christ and Christianity, Constantinople was the meeting-place of several ecumenical councils of which the second, in 381, the fourth, in 451, and the sixth, 680, assembled in the city (Welt der Bibel 2009, pp. 43–45).

With the spreading of Greek-Orthodox religion in a number of countries Constantinople emerged as a World City in the field of religion.

2. World City Rank: 7th–11th Centuries

In addition to the prime position of Constantinople in politics and religion another sector of society achieved excellence, the economic field – not only in commerce and long distance trade, but also in manufacturing on an artisanal base. This, together with the population increase of the city, the economy and the blooming culture led to historical World City rank from about the 7th to the 11th centuries.

Before that period commerce in the eastern Mediterranean area had been dominated by Syrian merchants (RUNCIMAN 1952, p. 90), contacts with the west were maintained via Constantinople. ABU-LUGHOD (1989, pp. 138–140) published a sequence of three maps showing the reticulation of trade-routes in the Mediterranean Sea and Central Asia for 737, 1212 and 1478. From the 7th until the 11th centuries the trade-routes were dominated by Byzantine merchants, Constantinople being the centre of mercantile connections on land and sea routes between Western Europe, Central and Western Asia.

Constantinople was also an attractive market of itself for luxury and consumer goods. The "court, the vast civil service, the central church organization, a large number of monks, of lawyers and professional men" (RUNCIMAN 1952, p. 91) was the clientele for luxuries.

And the general population had to be fed. In this connection the amount of imported grain from the northern coastlands of the Black Sea and from Egypt was important. Bulky goods, like grain, favoured the sea route, luxury goods were transported over land.

The weight of grain for Constantinople has been used – in comparison with Rome – for an estimation of the population of the city of Constantinople. For the 5th century KIRSTEN, BUCHHOLZ, KÖLLMANN (vol. I., p. 402) suggest 600000 inhabitants. But RUSSELL (1958/1961, p. 66) considers this figure as far too high and counted only 100000 inhabitants. RUNCIMAN (1952, p. 91) believes in 800000 during the highlight centuries of Constantinople.

For the year 622 the figure of 500000 inhabitants is given (BRONGER 2004, p. 168, based on CHANDLER, FOX 1974). This figure places Constantinople on second rank of all cities at the respective time, only a Chinese city, Chang'an, being a little larger (>500000).

For the year 1000 Constantinople scored first rank with a population of 450000 as the largest city on the globe at this time, with equal numbers in Córdoba (BRONGER 2004, p. 169, on the basis of CHANDLER, FOX 1974).

If the quoted figures can be relied on, Constantinople would – on the criterion of population alone – qualify as an historical World City.

There is no simple relation between the varying size of the Byzantine Empire and the population size of the capital city.
For the reign of Justinian I. (527–565) KIRSTEN, BUCHHOLZ, KÖLLMANN (vol. I., p. 402) mentioned 400 000 km², for the reign of Basileios I. (976–1025) 545 000 km².
It has to be taken into consideration that the Bubonic Plague, the Black Death (ABU-LUGHOD 1980, p. 127), had a great influence on the varying population of Constantinople. Whole quarters were wiped out in the densely populated inner parts of the city. After the Black Death struck in 1406 and 1435 the population is supposed to have dropped to 50 000 (KIRSTEN, BUCHHOLZ, KÖLLMANN, vol. 2, p. 108).

The dominating position of Constantinople in world trade during the last four or five centuries of the first millennium was not only secured by Constantinople's function as hub of international trade routes on land and sea (ABU-LUGHOD 1989, p. 138), but as much by the political position of the city as the capital of an empire. Not only that goods transported between distant lands were forced to pass the market of Constantinople for the benefit of Byzantine merchants, also a duty was imposed on ships passing through the Bosphorus – a heritage from Byzantium (RUNCIMAN 1952, p. 93).
Additionally Constantinople's strong economic, particularly commercial position was still enhanced by its function as a production centre of the silk industry.
After Nestorian monks had secretly brought silkworms from China – via the land route – to the Byzantine Empire, a silk industry grew up in Constantinople, serving an ample request of the city's court and high-ranking population (RUNCIMAN 1952, p. 90). Raw silk was imported from other places too and worked up into final products, some of them were exported (RUNCIMAN 1952, pp. 94–95). Besides, other important high-value goods, for instance spices, were re-exported to western and northern countries (RUNCIMAN 1952, p. 94). The silk industry of Constantinople was owned partly by the emperor himself, partly by private workshops organized in guilds (RUNCIMAN 1952, pp. 106–108).
It has been criticized that most modern scientific methods of dealing with World Cites or potential World Cities give preference to economic and sociological aspects and lack the aspect of culture as part of the excellence of World Cities.
The respective situation of Constantinople from the 7th to the 11th centuries is a fitting example for the importance of the cultural aspect. The monastic influence and the grandeur of the emperor's court were the basic impulse, mainly on ecclesiastic music and icons of Christian dignitaries, but there were

also literary and art circles and the achievements of Byzantine architecture in church buildings and monasteries should not be forgotten (HAUSSIG 1959, pp. 271–330). Besides, there was what has been called the infamous Byzantine life-style, another kind of culture.

The structure of the city of Constantinople had been laid out in the centuries following the building of the city walls of Constantine (306–337) and Theodosius II. (408–450). It incorporated ancient institutions of Roman times, fori (Constantini, Theodosii, Bovis, Arcadii), new ones were added. An additional residential quarter (Palace of Blachernae) was constructed for the Byzantine emperors, and cisterns (Aspar, Aetius, Motius) for the water supply of the population. Many churches and monasteries were erected not only on the western side of the Bosphorus, but also on the eastern side, thus including this area structurally in the city of Constantinople (JANIN 1964, maps 1, 3, 5, 6, 7, 11, 12; STEWIG 1964, p. 27-map).

The Great Land Wall was constructed in such a distance from the central city that even in late Ottoman times the area encircled by the wall had not been built-up completely, but was used for horticultural purposes.

As a centre of maritime transport harbours were important for Constantinople (MÜLLER-WIENER 1994). The coastal stretches bordering the Golden Horn and the Sea of Marmara near the entrance to the Bosphorus were the harbour sites of which those on the Sea of Marmara (Bukoleon, Julian, Contoscalion, Eleutherios) were open to southerly gales, but protected against the dominating north winds (JANIN 1964, map 1, pp. 225–244; STEWIG 1964, p. 27-map). The harbours on the Golden Horn (Bosporion, Neorion, Dionysios) were preferred by foreign merchants settling there and on the opposite side of the Golden Horn in their own quarters.

3.   Decline: 11th Century–1453

The decline of the Byzantine Empire happened in many ways and many fields: politically, territorially, economically, culturally and concerning the population of Constantinople.

One blow came from the Turkic tribes pushing westwards from Central Asia north and south of the Black Sea. In 1071 the Battle of Manzikert/Malazgirt in eastern Anatolia, lost by the Byzantine Empire, started the territorial reduction (PITCHER 1972, map 6). The Seljuks invaded Anatolia and organized their emirates in the 14th century (PITCHER 1972, map 7). One of these emirates, the most western one, was the homestead of the Ottomans who, in the course of history, managed to found an empire covering parts of Asia, Europe and North Africa. The emirate of the Ottomans expanded quickly. In 1326 they made the city of Bursa, in Northwest Anatolia, their first capital city and in 1360 – even before they transferred their capital to Edirne in 1365 – they advanced to the eastern, Anatolian side of the Bosphorus (PITCHER 1972, map 8).

In 1395 the Ottoman fortress of Anadolu Hisarı was built on the Anatolian coast of the Bosphorus in anticipation of the siege of Constantinople which happened 58 years later. When the Ottomans actually besieged Constantinople in 1453 they had already conquered and occupied most of the possessions of the Byzantine Empire in the Balkan lands (PITCHER 1972, map 11), though they suffered from an interregnum between 1402 and 1413 when Tamerlane/ Timurlenk invaded Anatolia.

The age of the Crusades, which started with the First Crusade in 1096 – it took the land route via Constantinople and Anatolia to the Holy Land – was on the whole detrimental to Constantinople though a fiery interest in the Orient was kindled in Western Europe which had positive effects on commerce with the east (ABU-LUGHOD 1989).

The Fourth Crusade, starting in 1204, was not directed towards the Holy Land, but ransacked Constantinople in 1204 and devastated the Byzantine capital. The remains of the Byzantine Empire evaded to Niceae/Iznik in Northwest Anatolia as capital and succeeded in regaining the much harassed Constantinople in 1261.

For the rest of the time to 1453 the Byzantine Empire was reduced more and more until only the immediate surroundings were left.

At first the two Italian city-states of Venice and Genoa and others (Pisa, Amalfi), dominating commerce and trade in the eastern and western Mediterranean Sea since the 11th century (ABU-LUGHOD 1989, pp. 102–134, maps on pp. 123, 138–140), though themselves competing heavily – Venice more in the east, Genoa more in the west – seemed to be helpful to the Byzantine Empire and Constantinople. However, the Byzantine Emperors being in financial distress because of the costly wars they had to fight with the aggressors, mostly the Ottomans, conceded – for money – commercial privileges, exemption from duties in the Byzantine Empire for the foreign merchants, who settled in Constantinople on the southern, later on the northern side (the Genoese) of the Golden Horn (STEWIG 1964, p. 27-map). The merchants of Venice received their quarter in 1082, those from Pisa in 1111, those from Genoa in 1152; those from Amalfi were the first, in the 11th century, to be located in a quarter of their own at the Golden Horn (KÜNZLER-BEHNCKE 1960, p. 53; JANIN 1964, pp. 245–260).

This means that foreign powers took over the international Orient trade, though at first through the organizations of their settlements in Constantinople. But, of course, the lure of direct contacts with the Orient from Venice and Genoa, enhanced by the effects of the Crusades, would not be withstood on the long run. HAUSSIG (1959, pp. 419–422) called Venice and Genoa the grave-diggers of the Byzantine Empire.

After the political defeat of the empire and the reduction of its territory to negligence the economic position of Constantinople was nihilated.

4.   Evaluation

The question is: can Constantinople be classified as a historical World City? Within the ultralong period of Constantinople bearing this name from 330 to 1453 the city was the political capital of an empire, the religious capital of a denomination and for a shorter time, from the 7th to the 11th centuries, the traffic hub of long range land and sea communication and the economic capital of the eastern Mediterranean and beyond, the largest city on the globe, according to its population size, and a top cultural centre. The range of influence covered – with varying extent – parts of three continents, Europe, Asia and Africa. In such a position Constantinople can rightfully be classified as a historical World City.

IV. Istanbul 1453–1920 : World City Rank and Decline

The reader of the preceding chapter having been informed in three sections about Constantinople's development to World City rank – the first section dealing with Constantinople's rise to World City rank – may be astonished not to find a similar section about Istanbul's rise to World City rank. As a matter of fact, the preparation for Istanbul's function as a capital of the Ottoman Empire proceeded outside that city between 1280 and 1453, during a period when Constantinople still existed as the capital of the shrinking Byzantine Empire.

About 1280 pasture lands were given by the rulers of Anatolia, the Seljuks, to a nomadic tribe in Northwest Anatolia, round Söğüt, not far from the present city of Iznik, on the border of the much reduced Byzantine Empire (SHAW 1976, pp. 9–14). The principality/emirate under the tribal chief Ertuğrul, the father of the name-giving Osman/Otman (1280–1324), covered in the beginning 1500 km² (MATUZ 1990, p. 32). Conquests commenced on both sides of the Sea of Marmara after the Dardanelles had been crossed about 1359 (SHAW 1976, pp. XIV–XV-maps).

Under Osman the territory amounted to 18 000 km² (MATUZ 1990, p. 32). Conquests continued on both sides of the Aegean Sea covering under Orhan (1326–1360) 75 000 km² (MATUZ 1990, p.34). The expansion went on in an amazing fashion attaining at the time of Murat I. (1360–1389) 260 000 km² (MATUZ 1990, p. 38). Beyazıt I. (1389–1402) topped in 1395 690 000 km² (MATUZ 1990, p. 44), holding large parts of Anatolia and the Balkans, thus making the principality not only an Anatolian, Asiatic power, but also a European one. As the consequence of the invasion of Tamerlane, the defeat in the Battle of Ankara in 1402 and the following interregnum from 1402 to 1413 (SHAW 1976, pp. 35–36), the territory was reduced – temporarily – to 340 000 km² (MATUZ 1990, p. 49).

The expansion was taken up again after 1413 in both the European and Asiatic theatres of war. At the time of Mehmet II. Fatih (1451–1481), the conqueror of Constantinople, the extent of the Ottoman territory amounted to 850 000 km² (MATUZ 1990, p. 49) on two continents – truly empire size.

The expansion is well documented by PITCHER (1972) in a series of maps (maps XI, XII, XIII, XVI, XVII).

It was not the territorial splendour alone that placed the state in an imperial position, much more its political and organizational structure.

Ertuğrul was a tribal chief: the decisions were made by a council of elders (SHAW 1976, p. 23).

Successful achievements were the transition from nomadic to settled conditions, the establishment of Bursa as the first capital of the Ottoman emirate in 1362 and the mastering of the conquered native, mostly Greek population. SHAW (1976, p. 23) believes that many Byzantine institutions were taken over and given an Asiatic and Islamic veneer.

The Ottoman emirate started on a local basis. But soon the regional and even the international dimensions had to be tackled. This could not be done by a single person or a small body of officials. So separate commanders were appointed for the Asiatic and European areas.

The transfer of the capital city from Bursa to Edirne in 1365 underlined that the Ottoman state had become a European power.

With the growing spatial dimensions of the state more and more different tasks had to be tackled (SHAW 1976, pp. 22–28).

At tribal times there were only horsemen as fighters. The condition of the adversaries required an infantry to be added to the Ottoman cavalry. So an army had to be created with commanders and officials/officers.

The spatial dimension of the state also demanded an administrational organization.

Already Orhan appointed a man not belonging to his family as vezir, i.e. chief minister (SHAW 1976, p. 24). In the course of time more vezirs were added for different tasks and other matters. Final decisions were made by the divan, an Imperial Council, presided over by the sultan (SHAW 1976, p. 25). The office of kadı, a Muslim judge, was institutionalized for juridical matters (SHAW 1976 pp. 26, 122). A hierarchy of ranks, outwardly recognized by the different number of horse-tails worn by the officials, evolved in connection with the Ottoman army and regional administration (SHAW 1976, p. 26). A special force of the military was organized, the Janissaries (SHAW 1976, p. 26).

The rapid expansion of the Ottoman state to empire size is proof of the effectiveness of the political organization.

The greatest achievement was perhaps the feudal organization of the state on the basis of fiefs (timar) combining regional hierarchization of agricultural, financial and military matters with bondage to the head of state (SHAW 1976, on many pages).

So a fully fledged organization of the widely spread state existed when in 1453, after the conquest of Constantinople by Mehmet II. Fatih Istanbul was ready to take over the function of capital city of the Ottoman Empire.

1. World City Rank: 1453–1683

This period has been called the apogee of the Ottoman Empire, comprising the reign of the two outstanding Ottoman sultans, Mehmet II. Fatih (1451–1481) and Süleyman I. The Magnificent (1520–1566) (SHAW 1976,p. 55).

Two remarkable events happened in their reigns, the first siege of Vienna in 1529 and the second siege of Vienna in 1683 – a date which fixes a turning point in Ottoman history. Both sieges were unsuccessful, but mark the farthest advance of the Ottomans into Europe, creating fear in remembrance of ancient invasions of Turkic groups into Central Europe (MATUZ 1990, pp. 119, 185).

The expansion of the Ottoman Empire continued. Spectacular acquisitions were: Serbia in 1459, Bosnia in 1463, the Peloponnesus (Morea) in 1458–1460, Syria in 1488, Irak, Palestine, Egyt in 1517, Mesopotamia and the coastlands of the Arabian peninsula, the Cyrenaica in 1521, Tripoli in 1551, Tunis in 1574, Hungary in 1526 (SHAW 1976, frontispiece map). The expansion is documented in a series of maps by PITCHER (1972, maps XVI, XVII, XIX, XXI, XXIII, XXIV).

Had the empire already been extended to 850 000 km² in the reign of Mehmet II. (1451–1481), it covered in the reign of Süleyman I. The Magnificent (1520–1566) 2 225 000 km² without vassal states (MATUZ 1990, p. 119). When vassal states like the Crimea (1475), Transylvania (1541), Wallachia (1393) and Moldavia (1504) are included the territory amounted to 3 500 000 km² (MATUZ 1990, pp. 129, 164). With this extension the Ottoman Empire was the largest state on the globe at that time (MATUZ 1990, p. 164) and a top political scorer of world rank though the age of discovery, America in 1492, Africa rounded in 1498, had enlarged the global dimension beyond the Mediterranean Sea and the Old World.

The Ottoman Empire, exercising its sovereignty over most divers landscapes, mountains and plains, villages, towns and cities, many peoples of different origin, speaking a multitude of languages and belonging to several races and religions, was a world of its own right.

Having attained sovereignty over the Holy Places in Arabia, the title of Caliph, as head of the world-wide Islamic community, is supposed to have been given to Sultan Selim I. (1512–1520) (SHAW 1976, p. 85; MATUZ 1990, p. 83). So the sultan in Istanbul was not only a political leader but also the religious leader of Islam. Istanbul continued to be the seat of the Greek Orthodox and Armenian Patriarchates.

The phenomenal growth of territory of the Ottoman Empire in the period from 1453 to 1683 was paralleled by a similar phenomenal growth of the city of Istanbul from a very low start. It is not surprising that the population of the city of Istanbul was down to 40 or 50 000 people after the siege, the conquest and the following pillage of Constantinople (KIRSTEN, BUCHHOLZ, KÖLLMANN 1956, vol. 2, p. 108). But the conqueror Mehmet II. (1451–1481) was – probably since a long time – determined to make Istanbul his capital city and was bent on peuplement. There is a detailed investigation about the filling-up of Istanbul with population (SCHNEIDER 1949; MANTRAN 1962, pp. 42–44). It is not only that Muslims and Turkish people from Anatolia were – partly by force – resettled in Istanbul, also Greek population from the southern Balkans suffered the same fate (STEWIG 1964, p. 41-map). The number of inhabitants of Istanbul increased rapidly. At the time of Süleyman I. The Magnificent (1520–1566) the population of Istanbul is supposed to have reached 500 000 (KIRSTEN, BUCHHOLZ, KÖLLMANN 1956, vol. 2, p. 108). In 1573 – according to a Venetian report – the population of Istanbul amounted to 300 000 (RUSSELL 1958/1961, p. 130.)

Due to the settlement of Christians (Greeks and Armenians) and Jewish population the contrast between Muslims and non-Muslims evolved. The comparatively high degree of non-endogenous people is not untypical of World Cities. According to MANTRAN (1962, pp. 44–47, map 5) the relation between

Muslims and non-Muslim was 58,1% to 41,89% in 1478. The respective data for 1530 to 1535 are 58,3% to 41,7%, for 1550 57,7% to 42,3%. For the end of the 17th century MANTRAN published the figure of 345–430 000 Muslims to 250–310 000 non-Muslims (MANTRAN 1962, pp. 44–47). For 1681 the total population has been evaluated at 800 000 (MANTRAN 1962, map 2; STEWIG 1964, p. 42, 46-map).

The population – Muslims and non-Muslims – clustered around their places of divinity, mosque, church, synagogue, and according to common spatial origin.

The relation of a city to other cities, its position on a rank scale based on numbers of inhabitants, is one criterion for the decision about World Cityness.

Constantinople reached top position – as the largest city on the globe – about the year 1000 A.D. with 450 000 people (BRONGER 2004, p. 169 on the basis of CHANDLER, FOX 1974).

Istanbul, during the period from 1453 to 1683 started from 200 000 people in 1500 – a comparatively high figure, considering that only 47 years had elapsed since the conquest of Constantinople – as number nine on the rank-scale, four Chinese cities – Beijing with 672 000 people – and in Europe Paris (225 000) being larger. About 1600 Istanbul had attained the second position with 700 000 inhabitants, only Beijing being a little larger (706 000). About 1700 – at the end of the respective period – Istanbul reached with unchanged 700 000 inhabitants first rank as the largest city on the globe, surpassing Beijing (>600 000) (BRONGER 2004, p. 169, on the basis of CHANDLER, FOX 1974). There is no doubt that Istanbul had reached historical World Cityness in the apogee of the Ottoman Empire, London (550 000) in fourth and Paris (530 000) in fifth place.

As an Islamic and Turkish capital city of the Ottoman World Empire the structure of Constantinople was re-modelled in the Oriental, common medieval pattern after 1453.

The most important structural elements were the palace of the sultan and the traditional shopping-centre, the bazaar (STEWIG 1964, p. 46, 48-map). Mehmet II. Fatih (1451–1481) had a first Eski Sarayı built in Istanbul in 1454, west of the Yeni Sarayı, the opulent residential quarter, the Topkapı Sarayı, the Seraglio Palace, on the tip of land between the Bosphorus, the Golden Horn and the Sea of Marmara, on the first hill, the site of ancient Byzantium (STEWIG 1996, p. 48-map), today a museum and important attraction for tourists.

The other important structural element was the bazaar. Mehmet II. had it built in 1455 (SHAW 1976, p. 59). Today the bazaar of Istanbul, with the two massively built bedestens, originally for the sale and storage of precious goods and for banking transactions, and the covered bazaar streets (Kapalı Çarşı), originally for the sale of goods, imported and/or produced on the spot by workshops, is as much a tourist attraction as the Topkapı Sarayı. The caravansaries (hans), originally for the management of long distance trade, having lost their functions are – though part of the bazaar area – not an attraction to tourists.

The re-modelling of Christian Constantinople took place – in an aesthetic way – by placing a number of mosque-complexes on the seven hills of the city – their numbering having been introduced in Byzantine times after the model of Rome (STEWIG 1964, p. 21-map):
- the Aya-Sofya-mosque, the main place of Byzantine divinity, only slightly changed by adding four massive minarets, on the first hill
- the Sultan-Ahmet-mosque, dating from 1617, as the Islamic main place of divinity, with six minarets, on the first hill
- the Nuruosmaniye-mosque from 1755 on the second hill
- the Valide-mosque from 1870 on the northern slope of the second hill
- the Beyazıt-mosque from 1500 on the western slope of the third hill
- the Şehzade-mosque from 1548 on the western slope of the third hill
- the Selimiye-mosque, originally a Byzantine monastery, on the sixth hill
- the Kahriye-mosque, originally a Byzantine monastery, on the sixth hill
- the Koca-Mustafa-mosque, from after 1453, on the seventh hill
   (STEWIG 1964, pp. 50–51).

By the placement of most of the grand historical mosque-complexes on hills the skyline of the old quarters of the city of Istanbul has been formed in an impressive and aesthetic way, to this day.

Ottoman architecture – with Byzantine influence – as a cultural achievement was brought to a level of world reputation by the many works of Mimar Sinan (1490/1491–1588), the architect of three sultans of the 1453–1683 period. Most of his works are in Istanbul, the most important one is the Şehzade-complex from 1551–1574 (GOODWIN 1971, pp. 196–283; GORYS 2003, p. 120).

With the enmassment of representative mosque-complexes Istanbul qualifies as a World City in and beyond the 1453–1683 period. The general recognition of this fact is still lacking.

Besides architecture the reigns of Mehmet II. Fatih (1454–1481) and Süleyman I. The Magnificent (1520–1566) were highlights of culture (SHAW 1976, pp. 142–149). "A wave of Muslim scholars flooded the centre of power" (SHAW 1976, p. 142). Religious thinking progressed, medicine, astronomy, mathematics. Historiographic and geographic literature, including maps of the known world by Piri Reis (died 1533), were widely distributed. In the 17th century Evliya Ġelebi was a great traveller who published his observations in his ten-volume Seyahatname, today an important source book for knowledge about the Ottoman Empire.

Besides, poetry was fashionable, divan literature for the educated classes in Istanbul and folk literature. In the 16th century the shadow play (karagöz) was developed.

The cultural role of Istanbul fitted-in well with the World City rank at the time.

The question has to be posed, if Istanbul when it was a World City between 1453 and 1683 on the basis of its political function, the size of the empire, the number of inhabitants and its cultural life, held an equivalent position as a hub of international communications.

In consequence of the age of discovery the economic interest of West European nations, Portugal, Spain, France, England, the Netherlands in turn, shifted – slowly – away from the Mediterranean Sea to the Atlantic Ocean. But commercial connections continued to be maintained between Europe, the Orient and Central Asia, Istanbul still holding an appropriate position of participation.

As long as several more or less independent emirates existed in Anatolia in the 14th century, in Seljuk times, the important land route, originally leading from Constantinople diagonally across the central plains, fell in decay (TAESCHNER 1924/1926; PITCHER 1972, map VII.). After the conquest of these emirates by the Ottomans the land route system of Anatolia – from Istanbul – was restored (MANTRAN 1962, map 2). Together with the land route system in the Balkans Istanbul regained the old position of Constantinople as traffic hub of connections, leading – on land – to Central Asia (INALCIK 1973, pp. 122–123-map; ABU-LUGHOD 1998, p. 140-map). Caravans of camels and dromedaries became the common means of land transport and were widely used (BRAUDEL 1986, pp. 530–531).

The Ottoman Empire having acquisitioned the sea boards not only of the Black Sea, but also of all sea boards of the eastern Mediterranean Sea, the state accrued to its political position as land power sea power qualities. For implementation a strong navy was created. Hayruddin Barbarossa (1466–1546) became Grand Admiral (SHAW 1976, pp. 96–102). With the force of sea power, which suffered heavy drawbacks, so in the Battle of Lepanto (1571) (SHAW 1976, pp. 178–179), the Black Sea and the Eastern Mediterranean became inland waterways of the

Ottoman state, which – by political decision – could be opened or closed to international and foreign mercantile activities, especially the straits, the Bosphorus and the Dardanelles.

The problem is if – or how much – Istanbul was the organisational centre of trade, particularly of trade with the Orient, Europe and Central Asia in the period between 1453 and 1683. There is little and uncertain information about this (INALCIK 1973, pp. 121–139). Definitely, Istanbul with its very large population was a centre of consumption and as much a centre of imports in many ways (MANTRAN 1962, pp. 185–213), of grain from the coastal areas of the Black Sea. MANTRAN (1962, pp. 211–213) published a long list about the provisioning of Istanbul in the second half of the 17th century. Foreign countries took part in the business. Commercial connections with the Orient, with Europe and Central Asia continued (ABU-LUGHOD 1989, p. 140-map). BRAUDEL (1986, pp. 526–528) believes that Istanbul was a centre for the exchange of bullion and coins of different metal content of gold and/or silver from various mints and this served well the finances of the state/sultans. It seems that the activities lay less in the hands of Ottoman merchants than in those of foreigners.

The seeds of decline of Istanbul and the Ottoman Empire were already planted in the period between 1453 and 1683 (INALCIK 1973, pp. 137–139; SHAW 1976, pp. 169–215).

When the Venetians and Genoese slowly lost their commercial dominance, other foreigners took over. In 1536 the first of the infamous capitulations (SOUSA 1933; NEBIOĞCU 1941) was agreed with France, privileges of free trade in the Ottoman Empire for payments to the sultan (MATUZ 1990, p. 122; but compare SHAW 1976, p. 177, who gives 1569). This was the first of the new western foreigners' intrusion in Istanbul and the Ottoman Empire. In 1580 England followed, in 1612 the Netherlands (MATUZ 1990, pp. 122, 157).

The Levant Company (WOOD 1935/1964; INALCIK 1973, p. 138) had been formed as a combination of several commercial companies, among them the Venice Company. The Levant Company took over large parts of the direct trade between western Europe and the Orient.

The new foreigners residing in Istanbul, the French, the English, the Dutch, later the Austrians, the Poles and the Russians (MANTRAN 1962, pp. 545, 583), enhanced the heterogeneity of Istanbul's population – a tendency not unfamiliar with World Cities.

Spatially the maritime traffic was more and more concentrated in the Golden Horn; the ancient ports on the coast of the Sea of Marmara were given up. In the Golden Horn, which turned out to be the major harbour and port of Istanbul, traffic was relatively heavy so that different landing stages were organized for the different sea routes (MANTRAN 1962, map 9; MÜLLER-WIENER 1994, pp. 37–74, 126–127). Kasımpaşa, on the northern side of the Golden Horn, became the shipyard and naval quarter of the Ottoman fleet.

Economic activities of Istanbul in the period from 1453 to 1683 do not seem to have been on the level of World City rank, compared with Istanbul's position in imperial politics, size of territory, number of population and culture.

2. Decline: 1683–1920

The date 1683 marks the year of the second unsuccessful siege of Vienna by the Ottomans. In 1920 the Ottoman parliament met for the last time in Istanbul. This was the end of Istanbul as political capital of the Ottoman Empire and – at the close of the First World War – the end of the Ottoman Empire as well.

Politically the decline is evident in a number of phenomena, one is the loss of territory of the Ottoman Empire and the hinterland of Istanbul. Several causes contributed to this development: the spreading of the ideology of nationalism and independence, first but not only among the conquered peoples, the uprisings and revolts in Anatolia, internal structural changes of the organization of the Ottoman Empire (the breakdown of the feudal system), the weakness and technological backwardness of the Ottoman military (SHAW 1976, on many pages).

Some of the important dates are:
- 1699: loss of Hungary and Transylvania to Austria
- 1774: independence of the Crimea
- 1830: independence of Greece
- 1878: independence of Romania, autonomy of Bulgaria
- 1908: independence of Bulgaria
- 1913: independence of Albania (SHAW 1976, pp. 300–301-map).

At the end of the First World War Syria and Lebanon became French mandates, Palestine, Transjordan and Mesopotamia British mandates. Egypt won autonomy in 1811, independence in 1922. Tripoli and Cyrenaica (Libya) were lost to Italy in 1912 (SHAW 1976, pp. 300–301-map).

At the end of the First World War the Ottoman state was reduced to Anatolia and – making things worse – the Treaty of Sèvres in 1920 demanded the splitting up of Anatolia: into a western portion on the Aegean Sea coast to

Greece, Southwest Anatolia to Italy, Southeast Anatolia to France. Had this plan been implemented it would have meant the obliteration of the Turkish state (SHAW 1976, pp. 300–301-maps). Istanbul would have lost its hinterland almost completely.

About 1700, the end of the 1435–1683 period, Istanbul had scored top rank of all cities on the globe with its population of about 700 000 (BRONGER 2004, p. 169, on the basis of CHANDLER, FOX 1974) as the splendid capital of the Ottoman Empire. In 1920, at the end of the First World War, Istanbul lost its function of capital with the breakdown of the Ottoman Empire. Ankara the inland city, was chosen as capital by Atatürk (STEWIG 1966). In 1927, when the first census of the Republic of Turkey appeared, the city of Istanbul (not the province) had 704 825 inhabitants (Devlet Istatistik Enstitüsü 2002, p. 42).

Between the two decisive dates, 1683 and 1920, Istanbul's population experienced contrasting developments.

On the one hand – in spite of the extreme territorial losses and the reduction of the range of the function as capital city – the population remained comparatively high, even increased temporarily: 1838: 547 000, 1886: 851 000, 1897: 903 000, 1906: 864 000, 1910: 855 000, 1913: 909 000 (SHAW, SHAW 1977, pp. 241–242). The explanation is that refugees, mainly Muslims, moved from the lost territories into the remaining Ottoman Empire and Istanbul. In the 20-year period between 1876 and 1896 845 000 refugees entered the Ottoman Empire (SHAW, SHAW 1977, p. 242).

This meant the increase of the Muslim population of the city. In 1878 the percentage of the Muslim population in Istanbul was 37,1% (Greeks: 17,5%, Armenians: 17,8%, Jews: 3,5%, foreigners 22,3%). In 1886 the percentage of the Muslim population in Istanbul amounted to 45,1% (Greeks: 17,9%, Armenians: 17,5%, Jews: 2,6%, foreigners: 15,1%)(SHAW, SHAW 1977, p. 242).

While normally the presence of deviant populations is an indicator of World City rank and of a city's far reaching range of influence, the refugees of Istanbul were unproductive citizens of their own country.

On the other hand Istanbul was surpassed by the growth of many other large cities on the globe. On the rank scale Istanbul dropped from first place in 1700 to third place in 1800 (570 000), kept third place in 1825 (675 000) and in 1850 (785 000), but was down to 16th place in 1875 (600 000) and fell out of the rank scale of the most populous 20 cities afterwards (BRONGER 2004, pp. 169–170).

Istanbul, no longer a World City – was now a regional centre. Even the many peace treaties in connection with the territorial losses (Karlowitz 1699,

Passarowitz 1718, Küçük Kaynarca 1774, Bucharest 1812, Edirne 1829, Berlin 1848, Paris 1856) were signed outside Istanbul (SHAW 1976; SHAW, SHAW 1977).

But cultural achievements continued after 1683, in the Tulip/Rococo period (1718–1730), when Ottoman intellectual awakening began (SHAW 1976, p. 235), and in the 19th century in the age of the Tanzimat (1839–1909) (SHAW, SHAW 1977, pp. 128–133).

It has been stated that the decline of Istanbul in the 1683–1920 period was evident in the extreme reduction of its range of competence as a political capital. The lost position as the top scorer in the international urban rank scale of city size by population was due to the growth of other large urban centres outside the Ottoman Empire at a time when Istanbul's population remained relatively high; but it was the refugees that made up part of the inhabitants of the city.

In the fields of economics and communications the decline of Istanbul was not less evident. The costly wars over a very long time had ruined the financial situation of the state. The balance of revenues and expenditures was continuously in the negative. From 1877 to 1906 under Sultan Abdülhamit II. (1876–1909) the public debt varied between 39 % and 59 % (SHAW, SHAW 1977, p. 226). Even before the final collapse of the Ottoman Empire the state was bankrupt in 1875 (MATUZ 1990, p. 246).

A Public Debt Commission/Dette Publique Ottomane was established the same year in Istanbul to negotiate financial problems. This resulted in serious influence of foreign powers (SHAW, SHAW 1977, pp. 221–226; MATUZ 1990, p. 246).

In spite of the disastrous and lasting financial situation, in spite of the long time prevalence of imports over exports and resulting deficits (SHAW, SHAW 1977, p.122), the head of state, the sultan, as an absolute monarch, had an opulent palace built, the Dolmabahçe, at the water, on the Bosphorus, to be able to move out of the ancient Topkapı Sarayı/Seraglio Palace (STEWIG 1964, p. 48-map) into a new architectural highlight of Istanbul.

The dependency on capitulations, which had started before 1683 (France 1536, England 1580, the Netherlands 1612) continued in an extended measure. Capitulations with France were renewed in 1740, with England in 1838 (MATUZ 1990, pp. 203, 231). Between 1740 and 1840 more foreign nations joined the capitulary regime in Istanbul and the Ottoman Empire: Austria (1747, 1771), Denmark (1756, 1841), Sweden and Norway (1849), Belgium (1838, 1839, 1840), Holland (1840), Prussia (1761), Spain (1782, 1840), Russia (1783, 1829, 1846), the U.S.A. (1830), Portugal (1843), Greece (1840) (NEBIOĞLU 1941, p. 23). The European countries having advanced in societal evolution and especially in industrialization Istanbul and the Ottoman Empire was now open to the full impact of European commercial domination, the more so as direct contacts with the Orient had already been established.

This was supported by the development of communications and transport technology. After the defeat of the Ottoman Empire in the Crimean War (Peace Treaty of Paris in 1856) the Black Sea – Istanbul's inland lake – and the straits (Bosphorus and the Dardanelles) were opened to international shipping. The Bosphorus became a transit shipping lane, especially since the English Cornlaws had been repealed in 1846 and grain from Russia was imported to England (STEWIG 1864, pp. 36–39). For Istanbul as a port city this meant loss of revenues.

The direct commercial connection of Europe with the Orient – evading Istanbul – was fostered by the opening of the Suez Canal in 1869 – crossing nominal Ottoman territory (STEWIG 1964, p. 32-map).

Had the influx of refugees into Istanbul increased the Muslim population (SHAW, SHAW 1977, pp. 241–242), the commercial activities of the western powers in the Ottoman Empire on the basis of capitulations brought more foreigners to Istanbul (MANTRAN 1962, pp. 552–583; SHAW, SHAW 1977, p. 242). Besides, the activities of the (Ottoman) minorities in Istanbul were promoted. In 1886 25 % of the Muslim population of Istanbul was engaged in trade and industry, 36 % of the Greek, 43 % of the Armenians and 33 % of the Jews (SHAW, SHAW 1977, p. 244), while 11 % of the Muslims worked in government and services, but only 0,04 % of the Greeks, 0,06 % of the Armenians, 0,04 % of the Jews (SHAW, SHAW 1997, p. 244).

All this meant that the heterogeneity of the population of Istanbul increased – remarkable for a capital city of regional importance. The dominance of the non-Muslim population in Istanbul in commerce and industry was strengthened.

The 19th century was for Istanbul and the Ottoman Empire the age of reform, the Age of the Tanzimat (1839–1909) (SHAW, SHAW, 1972, pp. 255–272), which had already started earlier, in the 18th century, when French officers and engineers – during the period of dominance of France in the Orient trade – were engaged in the modernization of the Ottoman army and the defences of the Bosphorus (SHAW 1976, pp. 251–252, 261–264). The New Order (Tanzimat) (MATUZ 1990, p. 224) brought deeply felt changes, political and economic, organizational and technological innovations to Istanbul and the Ottoman Empire.

Politically it looked as if Istanbul would become a city with a parliament, when according to the 1876 constitution (MATUZ 1990, pp. 236–238) an Ottoman parliament with political parties was organized. It met for the first time in the Dolmabahçe Palace in 1877 (SEGER, PALENCSAR 2006, p. 68). But it was dissolved in 1878, to be re-instituted in connection with the Young Turks Movement in 1908 (SHAW, SHAW 1977, pp. 255–258, 274–279).

The government was re-organized after the West European fashion with a prime minister and several ministries (SHAW, SHAW 1977 pp. 216–218). This government chose as location the old quarters of the city not far from the Topkapı Sarayı/Seraglio Palace, the long-time seat of the sultans.

But the embassies and consulates of the foreign powers preferred a different location, opposite Eminönü, on the northern side of the Golden Horn, in Pera (and Galata), where the new Istanbul, the modern, western Istanbul developed and where the foreigners and minorities lived on and around the Grande Rue de Pera, the İstiklal Caddesi of today.

Modern banks settled in Galata, today Karaköy, below Pera, next to shipping companies at the side of the Bosphorus.

The Grande Rue de Pera evolved in the 19th century as a shopping street with a new type of retail institution, the department store, imported from the West, with elegant Western offerings, creating competition for the ancient bazaar. It was the new clientele of foreigners and the wealthy minorities that was attracted (TIMOR 2004; STEWIG 2009, pp. 40–41).

The Ottoman Empire was penetrated by foreign powers economically in a quasi-colonial way. Foreign companies did not start centrally, from Istanbul, but regionally, from several port cities on the coast of Anatolia, from Izmir, Adana, Trabzon, and from the Greek coast, Selanik (Thessaloniki) and Kavalla (STEWIG 1964, p. 34-map). This meant a great loss for Istanbul. However, the so-called Baghdad railway, built by German initiative – but not completed before the end of the Ottoman Empire – started from Istanbul (SHAW, SHAW 1977, p. 227).

The great road from Istanbul into the Balkans and to Central Europe decayed when the territory of the Ottoman Empire was reduced. In 1837 the road could no longer be used by wagons (JIREČEK 1877, p. 137; STEWIG 1964, p. 35). Instead a steamship line was opened on the Danube from Vienna to Istanbul in 1830 and other shipping lines through the Mediterranean Sea, so in 1837 from Trieste to Istanbul (JIREČEK 1877, p. 137; STEWIG 1964, p. 35).

Economically it appeared as if Istanbul was becoming an industrial city in late Ottoman times with successful foundations of several modern factories along the upper Golden Horn and also on the northern Bosphorus, at the Anatolian side, making use of raw materials of the country (tobacco, leather, wool, silk), producing for the army of the sultan (CLARK 1994, but compare MATUZ 1985). Modern weapons, rifles and battleships, were bought abroad (SHAW, SHAW 1977, pp. 226, 236; MÜLLER-WIENER 1968).

Technical innovations for modern communication were introduced in Istanbul, steamships and harbour works, postal and telegraphic service, a rack-railway running in a tunnel, trams, gas, electricity, a metal bridge across the Golden Horn (SHAW, SHAW 1977, pp. 226–230), all with ample participation of foreigners and the minorities.

Another field of great importance was the reform of education (SHAW, SHAW 1977, pp. 106–113, 249–252). It meant the beginning of secular education, not systematically for all, but as a juxtaposition to traditional, religious, Islamic education, in the form of several educational institutions, specialized schools and a university. Again foreign powers participated.

The American Protestant Robert College was founded in 1863, the French Galata Sarayı in 1868. In the main, the specialized schools were created for the mastering of the many new tasks in society (SHAW, SHAW 1977, pp. 112–113 – long list).

One is tempted to ask the question if all those innovations, which can be summarized under the heading of westernization, were an asset or a liability for Istanbul and the Ottoman Empire, a liability because the traditional way of living was being displaced, an asset because the standard of living was raised.

The answer – in connection with the subject of World Cities and Istanbul's position as a past or future World City – is different: Istanbul, after having lost its World City rank, was put in a position not to fall too much behind the development of large cities elsewhere. Westernization of Istanbul in the 1883–1920 period produced the pre-conditions for future developments to a World City.

3. Evaluation

Constantinople attained World City rank from the 7th to the 11th centuries at a time when the age of discovery and had not yet begun and its range of competence as a political capital of empire size covered parts of southeastern Europe, southwestern Asia and northern Africa.

It is a peculiarity of history that Istanbul's range of competence as the capital of the Ottoman Empire had been laid out at a time when the city of Constantinople still existed. When Istanbul moved in 1453 into the functions of political capital of the Ottoman Empire it reached World City rank without much delay, though the (Old) World had been widened by addition of the New World.

Between 1453 and 1683 Istanbul surpassed all other cities on the globe in numbers of inhabitants, economic importance in (the Orient) trade and cultural splendour during the reign of the two most competent sultans, Mehmet II. Fatih (1451–1481), the conqueror of Constantinople, and Süleyman I. The Magnificent (1520–1566).

The loss of Istanbul's World City rank, after 1863, which began before that date, and the down-grading to regional centre happened within the frame-work of the emerging contrast between developed and under-developed, respectively developing countries in the world in modern times.

The decline of Istanbul, though the city remained the capital of the (shrinking) Ottoman Empire until the end of the First World War, was due to political and economic developments outside the Ottoman Empire and Istanbul, the state could not keep pace with. But the period of decline was also marked by a wave of westernization, the Tanzimat in the 19th century and forerunners. This prevented Istanbul from falling too much behind and this laid the pre-condition for renewed up-grading in the future.

V. Istanbul 1920–2010: Decline and Rise to World City Rank

When at the end of the First World War the Ottoman Constitutional Monarchy with its parliament, which met until 1920 in Istanbul, was dissolved (SHAW, SHAW 1977, p. 347) and the Turkish Republic with its parliament, the Grand National Assembly, was constituted in Ankara in 1921 (SHAW, SHAW 1977, p. 350) profound negative impacts on Istanbul began.

Had the range of political competence of Istanbul before 1920, though reduced, still covered some parts of the Balkans, Southwest Asia and North Africa, it was curtailed by the Treaty of Sèvres in 1920 (PADEL 1921) to the peninsula of Anatolia and even there the interests of foreign powers (Greece, Italy, France, Britain) had to be acknowledged. Though part of the regulations of the Treaty of Sèvres was mitigated by the Treaty of Lausanne in 1923 (SHAW, SHAW 1977, pp. 365–369) the agreement with Greece about the compulsory exchange of Greek and Turkish populations had an additional detrimental effect.

The invasion of Greece into western Anatolia, Turkish homeland territory (SHAW, SHAW 1977, p. 342), was another blow to the new Turkish Republic and Istanbul, though at first members of the Greek minority remained in the city.

1. Istanbul 1920–1980: Decline

The decline of Istanbul after 1920 was initiated by the transfer of the function of capital city from Istanbul to Ankara in 1923. It was not only politically that Istanbul suffered but culturally and economically as well. The government employees and the foreign diplomatic services were withdrawn, though several embassy and consulate buildings remained as summer residences of the diplomats. But, of course, with the dismissal of the sultan and his entourage Ottoman splendour, once on a fickle financial basis, was gone. Many of the palaces of the sovereign and the high-ranking officials stood empty, were – in the course of time – turned into museums.

This appearance of Istanbul created for ORHAN PAMUK (2003) the mood of melancholy and tristesse (hüzün), which he rendered in his novel/documentary about the city in his youth (STEWIG 2006).

Another setback was the change of population structure of Istanbul. The foreigners left. When the new state of Israel had been founded in 1948 many Jews left Istanbul (ŞEN, AKAYA, ÖZBEK 1998, pp. 189–192). During the First World War the Armenians of the Ottoman Empire were extinguished. The Greek minority was attacked in Istanbul in 1955 by the mob and this led to emigration of many members of the Greek community (ŞEN, AKAYA, ÖZBEK 1998, pp. 187–189). Consequently the heterogeneity of Istanbul's population was reduced in a great extent, the pre-condition for World City rank by the presence of heterogeneous population was minimized.

The Armenians, the Greeks, the Jews and the foreigners had been the economically most active groups. Their loss hampered the economic development of Istanbul and Turkey in a massive way.

The policy of the new Turkish Republican government in Ankara disfavoured Istanbul, suspecting the city of the old Levantine tradition.

All scanty resources of the Republic were directed to building the town of Ankara into a capital city.

The new government was keen on promoting industrialization without help from abroad – after the model of the Soviet Union – because of the bad experience of the infamous capitulations. The state – not private enterprise – organized the creation of heavy industry. With the entrepreneural minorities gone the state had to take the initiative.

Two banks, the Sümer Bank in 1933 and the Eti Bank in 1935, were founded in Ankara (SHAW, SHAW 1977, pp. 391–392) for the organization of industry.

The manufacturing plants were not located in Istanbul – still the largest consumer agglomeration of the country – but in the areas of the raw materials (coal, cotton, iron ore) in the provinces of Turkey; Istanbul was left out in the cold.

The economic policy of the Turkish government changed several times until 1980, due to different election results and different party intentions.

After the single-party era ended in 1950 – the Republican People's Party had allowed only a state economy (etatism) – the competition of parties began and this led to the revival of private enterprise. Istanbul had its share of this positive development.

Turkey – a closed shop – was opened a little to imports; this again was favourable for Istanbul. The new economic policy of import-substitution – since 1963 (AMELUNG 1989; SCHUBERT 1996, p. 33) – kindled an industrialization process in Istanbul as the biggest consumer agglomeration of the country (STEWIG 1964, p. 67).

Istanbul grew to become the unrivalled largest industrial city of Turkey. In 1960 it accounted for 25% of all manufacturing activities in Turkey (TÜMERTEKIN 1961, p. 43). In 1982 it had 47,4% of all manufacturing enterprises and 32,5% of all factory workers (ÖZGÜÇ 1986/1987, p. 54; TÜMERTEKIN 1972, p. 57).

However, this positive development was no contribution to Istanbul as a potential World City. The products were meant for the national Turkish market; there was only a limited sale abroad. Yet endogenous Turkish enterprise replaced the losses of the economically active minorities of Istanbul.

After the Second World War the mechanization of agriculture in Anatolia with the help of the Marshall-Plan as a push-force and the industrialization of Istanbul as a pull-force brought an enormous amount of migrants to the city.

In 1935: 43,14% of the people of Istanbul were born in another province or abroad, in 1945: 50,85%, in 1950 46,93%, in 1955: 54,32%, in 1960: 56,67%, in 1965: 58,95%, in 1970: 63,42%, in 1975: 55,03% and in 1980: 61,78% (Devlet Istatistik Enstitüsü 2002, p. 44).

Consequently the number of inhabitants of Istanbul – the city, not the province – increased from 1927: 704 825, to 1935:758 488, to 1940: 815 638, to 1945: 908 050, to 1950: 1 002 085, to 1955: 1 297 372, to 1960: 1 506 040, to 1965: 1 792 071, to 1970: 2 203 337, to 1975: 2 648 006, to 1980: 2 909 455 (Devlet Istatistik Enstitüsü 2002, p. 42).

This looks like the fulfilment of a pre-condition for the rise to World City rank, but the functional background was lacking.

In 1959 real World Cities had reached already 13 138 000 inhabitants (Tokyo) and even São Paulo as the twentieth city in this rank order counted 2 572 000.

In 1970 Tokyo was again top scorer with 24 113 000, Manila as twentieth city had 4 831 000. In 1980 Tokyo was again first of twenty Mega Cities with 28 697 000, Chicago twentieth with 6 060 000 (BRONGER 2004, pp 172–173, on the basis of CHANDLER, FOX 1974). Cities in developing countries were already on the march forward to Mega Cities.

Most of the migrants that went to Istanbul were poor farmers or agricultural labourers from the countryside, unskilled or semi-skilled, and most of them drifted into the informal sector of the city economy, if they found work at all; illiteracy, especially among women, was high. But still, they preferred life in Istanbul to return to their village (SARAN 1974, p. 359).

The built-up area of Istanbul expanded by these migrants who settled in gecekondu areas, the largest one in Zeytinburnu in 1950, 51% (SEGER, PALENCSAR 2006, p. 87), just outside the Great Land Wall, near the Sea of Marmara, and in Gaziosmanpaşa, at the upper Golden Horn (TÜMERTEKIN 1970/1974, p. 331).

This new type of settlement got hold of the periphery of the city of Istanbul: the huts built overnight with primitive equipment and help of neighbours from the same village.

It would be unjust to call the gecekondu evler slums, though electricity, water and drainage were mostly lacking, in the beginning. In the course of time the settlements were up-graded. They were areas for the adjustment to city life (SUZUKI 1966).

To consider the gecekondu evler of Istanbul as detrimental to the image of a World City and the rise to World City rank is inappropriate. The Mega Cities of developing countries of the time – and today – are full of squatter areas, of shanty towns, bidonvilles, favelas, barriadas, villas miseria, callampas, clandestine quarters (BÄHR, JÜRGENS 2005, p. 272).

The growth of the lower social class in Istanbul is – though ethically not to be appreciated – obviously a pre-condition for the rise to World City rank, in line with other great cities that have already attained World City status.

2. Istanbul 1980–2010: Rise to World City Rank

a Introductory Remarks

About the 1980s the paradigm of World City research changed. Before, the monographic and idiographic approach dominated as has been already stated. Since then the emphasis of research was laid on the economic approach: the most important criterion for the designation World City was a city's function as a (global) financial centre. So in connection with Istanbul an attempt has to be made to find out if Istanbul is a (global) financial centre.

Before this procedure an investigation seems necessary which has been – as far as I can see – lacking with the economic approach to the subject of World Cities: the delineation of the pre-conditions for the emergence of financial centres as World Cities. A hint at globalization is insufficient. The political conditions for the possibility of impacts of globalization – different in the countries – have to be explained.

b   The New Economic Policy in Turkey since the 1980s

The beginning of the new economic policy in Turkey (STEWIG 2000, pp. 12–22, 223–231) has not in the first place to do with the military coup of 1980 – it started shortly before 1980 – but much more with the disastrous financial situation of the Turkish Republic – near state bankruptcy because of extensive trade and budget deficiencies. The International Monetary Fund (IMF) and the World Bank were only ready to provide new credits if a number of compulsory monetary/financial conditions were observed by the Turkish Republic.

The policy was drafted by Turgut Özal before 1980 and later implemented by him as a member of the new military/civilian government.

Privatization and liberalization are only two, but fundamental notions of the new policy.

The dire financial situation of Turkey was the legacy of several changes of economic policy since the foundation of the Republic in 1923 (SHAW, SHAW 1977, pp. 405–413). The economically active and financially potential minorities of Istanbul gone, after the First World War, the state had to organize the economy and particularly industrialization – outside Istanbul. So as long as the single-party regime existed in Turkey, the state ruled in a planned way the economy. When the single-party regime ended in the national elections of 1950, the period of reduction of state influence and growth of private economic initiative began.

The next period of a new economic policy in Turkey before 1980 was marked by import-substitution, which brought for Turkey and for Istanbul an industrialization-push of textiles and other consumer goods. In spite of placing the production process a step backwards by importing raw materials or semi-manufactured products and reserving the final stages to Turkish industrialists, the disastrous financial situation of the state could not be remedied.

The economic policy had as one of its aims the further reduction of state influence on the economy by privatization of state enterprises. Though the emergence of big holding companies dates back in Turkey to the 1920s (BUĞRA 1994, p. 57), the lack of Turkish capital necessitated the opening of the country – strictly avoided before – to foreign investors. In many branches of the economy – especially in Istanbul – joint-ventures mushroomed. This necessitated the liberalization of the financial market in Turkey to attract investors.

Though banks had already been founded in the Ottoman Empire in Istanbul – the Osmanlı Bankası in 1856, the Ziraat Bankası in 1888 and a stock-exchange in 1864 – the financial market in modern Turkey needed promotion. In 1985 a new stock exchange was opened in Istanbul (-Istinye). Foreign exchange operations and international capital movements were entirely liberalized in 1989 (ÖZYILDIRIM, ÖNDER 2008, p. 233-table).

All this put the Turkish economy and Istanbul as its economic capital on a new financial footing, opened the country and Istanbul to global influences and the impacts of globalization.

c   Istanbul as a Financial Centre

In any modern society financial transactions are today conducted by banks, of which several types exist: universal banks, depository banks, investment banks, issueing banks, private and state banks, and others.

In Istanbul's past wholesale buying and selling, credit arrangements, long distance maritime and caravan transports, were managed by merchants residing – having their offices – in the inner section of the bazaar, the bedesten. Modern banks appeared in Istanbul for the first time in the late Ottoman period, state banks with partly private capital, and private banks.

When the Turkish Republic was founded in 1923 several state-owned banks cared for the banking business (İş Bankası 1924, Türk Sanayi ve Maadin Bankası 1925, Emlak Kredi Bankası 927, Iller Bankası 1933, Sümer Bankası 1933, Eti Bankası 1935) (SHAW, SHAW 1977, pp. 391–392).

The new economic policy was an instigation for the founding of new, mostly privately owned banks and the invasion of foreign banks or branch offices of foreign banks.

However, in the course of time quite a number of privately-owned banks failed, so that the exact number of banks in Turkey is uncertain. A specialty is the existence of two or three interest-free banks, practising Islamic banking.

According to ÖZYILDIRIM, ÖNDER (2008, p. 232) in the year 2000 61 commercial banks operated in Turkey of which 18 were development and investment banks. After a number of (private) bank failures there existed in 2006 51 banks, 3 public, 14 foreign, 13 non-commercial and 4 interest-free/participation banks (http://en.wikipedia.org/w/index.php?title=List_of_banks_in_Turkey&printable=yes).

Istanbul's status as a (global) financial centre cannot be established by a list of existing banks. Important is the relation of Istanbul as a financial centre to other financial centres. This requires an extensive statistical basis for measurement, which is not easy to get.

Since a short time such a basis is provided by the Z/Yen Group, published in September 2009; it is the Global Financial Centres Index (CFCI) (6, 2009). It is a collection of evaluations/assessments from 1802 financial experts about 75 financial centres over a two year period, collected online, resulting in ratings and ranks. Rank number one was achieved by London (rating 790). Istanbul scored rank 72 of 75 financial centres, rating 442, New York rank number two, rating 774. The exceptional feature is not that Istanbul attained only a low rank, the outstanding feature is that Istanbul is on the list.

In connection with World City research a warning is revealed by a close look at the list. The following financial centres scored the following ranks and ratings: Jersey 14 (640), Guernsey 15 (638), Isle of Man 25 (609), Cayman Islands 26 (608), Bermudas 28 (597), British Virgin Islands 33 (584), Bahamas 48 (551) and Gibraltar 51 (543). There is not the least doubt that these financial centres are not World Cities, but off-shore centres. This fact makes it quite clear that the criterion of high rank among financial centres does not necessarily mean that we have to do with a World City. This is an argument against the one-sided economic approach. If the off-shore centres are deducted from the list, Istanbul would probably rank a little higher.

There are more ways of establishing Istanbul's position as a financial centre and a World City. This is the GaWC's (Globalization and World Cities Research Group) roster of World Cities, also called the Loughborough Group (BEAVERSTOCK, TAYLOR, SMITH 1999). The approach is expanded. More World Cities or potential World Cities are included in the investigation. And it is taken account of the fact that banks have to do with business administration firms, summerizingly called producer services, including accounting, advertising, legal services and banking. Besides, in each of these classes a distinction has been made between prime, major and minor centres (BEAVERSTOCK, TAYLOR, SMITH 1999, pp. 452–455). Besides, a hierarchy of World Cities is established distinguishing between Alpha (22), Beta (24) and (15) Gamma World Cities, i.e. 61 World Cities in all, according to values 1 to 12.

In the accountancy class Istanbul does not appear; in the advertising class Istanbul scored major rank; in the banking class Istanbul achieved minor rank; in the legal services class Istanbul again reached minor rank.

Among the Alpha, Beta and Gamma scale of World Cities Istanbul was given the lowest rank, Gamma World City (with four values) (cp. GERHARD 2004, p. 8), together with such cities as Barcelona, Berlin, Budapest, Copenhagen, Hamburg, Manila, Miami, Montreal.

There is still another way of assessing the position of Istanbul as a financial centre and World City: the aspect of connectivity to London (HALL 2001/2008 pp. 68–69).

Again the classes of accountancy, advertising, law and banking have been chosen. Compared with 54 other cities the percentage level of linkages to London have been investigated.

In the class of accountancy with percentages between 93 (Paris) and 33, Istanbul (and Prague) scored 33; in the class of advertising with percentages between 90 (New York) and 0 (Osaka) Istanbul scored 62; in the class of law services with percentages between 68 (New York) and 0 (Copenhagen) Istanbul scored 3; in the class of banking and finance with percentages between 95 (New York) and 0 (Minneapolis) Istanbul scored 21.

Again Istanbul does not belong to the top rank – which could not be expected – but is not out of the assessment list of important financial linkages. So Istanbul – though on a low level – can be classed as (global) financial centre.

It is a commonplace that in World Cities a concentration of offices of many kinds is typical in a location which is architecturally characterized by highrise tower buildings, forming a peculiar skyline, different from almost every other part of the city. This – being the case in Istanbul too – is a trait which is entirely in line with World City rank. The emergence of such a concentration in Istanbul was fostered in great extent by the conditions created by the new Turkish economic policy since the 1980s (BERKÖZ 1998/2000; ÖZDEMIR 2002; BERKÖZ, EYUBOĞLU 2007). The Turkish economy boomed, experienced only short depression, and foreign direct investments flowed into the country. Istanbul profited immensely.

The multitude of new offices all belong to the tertiary economic sector, the service sector. There is the group of economic branches for which the acronym FIRE is being used, comprising finance (banking), insurance, real estate; investment and holding companies may be added, and there is the group of economic branches summarized as producer services, comprising advertising, computer services, accounting, offices of lawyers and notaries (BERKÖZ, 1998, p. 78).

Already in the 1990s, the office concentration in Istanbul contained 86 % of all business headquarters, 74,6 % of all finance and insurance companies and 62,0 % of all real estate companies of Turkey (BERKÖZ 1998, p. 78).

The procedure of operations, which uses modern communication technology, demands ample office space. As long as back office activities dominate and face-to-face transactions are unimportant, high-rise office constructions are architecturally feasible and lead to skyscraper buildings.

There exists a statistical account of the development of multi-storey buildings in the province of Istanbul – this actually refers only to the city of Istanbul – between 1984 and 2000. The number of buildings with ten and more storeys increased from 978 in 1984 to 6710 in 2000 (Devlet Istatistik Enstitüsü 2001, p. 401). Admittedly the share of high-rise hotel buildings north of the Taksim square and the share of high-rise apartment houses in many parts or Istanbul, even in the periphery, is unknown, but no doubt the largest share goes to the office concentrations.

In the traditional part of Istanbul the location of managerial activities – with face-to-face transactions – was the bazaar. Under the influence of westernization the location moved in the 19th century to Galata (Karaköy) and Pera (İstiklal Caddesi) with modern office buildings of limited height. Another move northwards began – slowly – in early Republican times. With the boom-years since the 1980s the expansion continued northwards from Şişli via Mecediyeköy, Gayrettepe and Levent to Maslak (SEGER, PALENCSAR 2006, pp. 139–140), accompanied by a shopping-centre axis (STEWIG 2009) and a metro/underground rail track (STEWIG 2006). This combination is typical of World Cities and qualifies Istanbul as a World City. The two Bosphorus bridges from 1973 and 1988 nearby and the inner urban motorway system (STEWIG 2006) enhance the accessibility to the area and several posh hotels and apartment houses revaluate the reputation of the site.

It is remarkable that office concentrations with high-rise buildings have also invaded the Anatolian side of the Bosphorus, next to two motorway junctions, in Altunizade and in Kozyatağı (ÖZDEMIR 2002, p. 251). Kozyatağı is the junction of the E5 with the TEM (Trans European Motorway). Even foreign firms moved to the place (Procter and Gamble, Colgate-Palmolive, Unilever, Citybank) (ÖZDEMIR 2002, p. 251). Cheaper building plots, less traffic congestion, improved accessibility probably caused the locational decision in favour of the site. In Altunizade the transfer of the headquarters of one of the large Turkish conglomerates, the Koç Holding Company, served as the forerunner (ÖZDEMIR 2002, p. 251).

To sum up: as a (global) financial centre Istanbul is a World City on a low level of activities, but for its structural and architectural appearance the city can well compete with other high-ranking World Cities.

d   Social Polarization in Istanbul

The group of World City researchers who are economistically minded and believe that global financial functions are the prerogative criteria for World Cities has also members who believe that a certain social structure of a city's population is no less typical and important (SASSEN 2000, 2006; cp. GERHARD 2004). The effects of globalization have expanded not only economically high-ranking managerial and technological occupations in great differentiation, but also largely increased low-income population working – if working at all – in the informal economy, the quaternary sector.

It is rather difficult to get wholesale statistical information about social polarization. For Istanbul attempts have been made by spatial differentiation of high- and low-income groups and occupational profiles in maps (GÜVENÇ 2006, pp. 207 208; SEGER, PALENCSAR 2006, p. 166).

The contrast in Istanbul between long existing gecekondu areas on the one hand and gated communities and gentrification – especially since the 1980s – on the other hand speaks for itself. The different forms of housing are indicative of social polarization.

α Mass Housing

Two phenomena of mass housing may be distinguished in Istanbul, one roughly before 1980, the other roughly since 1980. The first got to do with gecekondu evler (SUZUKI 1966; TÜMERTEKIN 1970/1971, 1972; SARAN 1974; KARPAT 1976; KEYDER 1999; STEWIG 2000).

The background is the mainly domestic migration in Turkey from rural to urban areas which slowly began after the end of the Second World War when mechanization of agriculture started with the help of the Marshall-Plan. Many small-scale farmers lost their existence and migrated to cities, especially Istanbul, in the hope of finding work there. This was the push from the rural side. The increased industrialization particularly in Istanbul, in the period of import-substitution economic policy before 1980 – compare BERKÖZ 1998, p. 339-graph – was the pull-force in Istanbul.

The unskilled and semi-skilled migrants belonged to the low-wage group of the population. This is why they had to care for their housing – the gecekondu evler – themselves. They settled as a mass phenomenon in the periphery of the city of Istanbul near the suburban areas of industrialization (TÜMERTEKIN 1970/1971) in Zeytinburnu (SEGER, PALENCSAR 2006, p. 87), outside the Great Land Wall, not far from the Sea of Marmara, in Gaziosmanpaşa, beside the industrial establishments on both sides of the upper Golden Horn, and in Beykoz, on the Anatolian side of the Bosphorus beside earlier factories from late Ottoman times.

It is interesting that KEYDER (1999, pp. 143–159) believes that due to the increased industrialization of Istanbul in the import-substitution period, i.e. before 1980, an emerging middle class was already noticeable – a development in line with the formation of industrial society (STEWIG 2000).

The other phenomenon of mass housing in Istanbul started even before the new economic policy set in powerfully (STEWIG 2000) in the form of the co-operative movement, which – though older – boomed after the Mass Housing and Investment Administration had been founded in 1984. New types of housing, multi-storey apartment houses, began to replace the areas of gecekondu evler more and more. The creation of a Toplu Konut Fonu, a Mass Housing Fund, which offered subsidized credit, allowed the construction of large and high-rise housing complexes with apartments for owners and renters.

This also meant a change of social attitudes, the withdrawal from the traditionally secluded family-life – a change in the direction of adopting universal, cosmopolitan behaviour.

Today the extensive periphery of the city of Istanbul is dominated by innumerable areas with forests of housing towers – an appearance not exceptional for World Cites.

β Gated Communities

The new economic policy in Turkey since the 1980s resulted in an economic boom, with few interruptions. Istanbul was the place for the re-organization of the economy of the country and its outside relations. The tertiary sector blossomed; it increased in a high degree (BERKÖZ 1998, p. 339-graph). Consequently the share of high-income population in the many branches of the tertiary sector increased too. This was the economic background for the emergence of gated communities (KEYDER 1999; GÖVENÇ, IŞIK 2002/2006); OZUS, DÖKMECI, KIROĞLU, EGDEMIR 2007; GENIŞ 2007; ESEN, RIENIETS 2008; PALENCSAR, STRMENIK 2010).

There are estimations that in Istanbul today more than 650 (!?) gated communities exist (GENIŞ 2007, p. 776; ESEN, RIENIETS 2008, p. 84). The gated communities are social enclaves, small and large residential areas of fairly high income population ranging from top level industrialists and businessmen to upper middleclass people like managers, lawyers, doctors (GENIŞ 2007, p. 795).

It has been maintained that it was not in the first place the search for security that called for gating measures (PALENCSAR, STRMENIK 2010, p. 23), but the longing for prestige living places where a posh life-style can be practised and for a pleasant environmental scenery. Some gated communities began as second homes on the coast of the Sea of Marmara and on both sides of the Bosphorus (ESEN, RIENIETS 2008, p. 84).

Besides security measures – electronic surveillance equipment and guardsmen – the infrastructure of the compounds is important: gardens, swimming pools, playgrounds, retail shops, schooling and sports facilities (GENIŞ 2007, p. 776).

The constructional and architectural types vary from single, hotel-like, vertical housing towers (PALENCSAR, STRMENIK 2010, pp. 22–23) in the city, where building plots are expensive, which leads to the combination of gated communities with modern, mall-type shopping-centres (STEWIG 2009, p. 103), and very large, horizontal gated communities in the outer periphery of Istanbul (PALENCSAR, STRMENIK 2010, p. 22-map), practically satellite towns, entirely residential in character, without working places, except for service personal (gardeners, house-keepers, nannies).

Gated communities in Istanbul are not only to be found in the coastal regions, but in the wooded interior of Istanbul province as well, where there is more and cheaper space for spreading-out.

The constructional and architectural types vary from opulent villas and semi-detached houses to terraced housing in individual styles (PALENCSAR, STRMENIK 2010, pp. 25–26).

No doubt, the existence of gated communities aggravates the segregation of the city and its population. This may be regretted from the social point of view. But it is none the less a trait of World Cities.

γ Gentrification

The phenomenon of gentrification (UZUN 2001, 2003; ERGUN 2004; YÜCESOY 2008) is the up-grading of mostly densely populated inner city areas. The best researched examples in Istanbul are Cihangir and Kuzguncuk, on opposite sides of the lower Bosphorus, Cihangir on a slope north of the Golden Horn, with a panoramic view of the southern entrance to the Bosphorus, Kuzguncuk on the Anatolian side in a valley opening to the Bosphorus (UZUN 2001, 2003). Besides these two there are minor signs of gentrification in Ortaköy on the Bosphorus and Fener and Balat on the Golden Horn. (ERGUN 2004).

Cihangir belongs to the old parts of the city of Istanbul, both Cihangir and Kuzguncuk have been settled since the 15th century. Both have to do with change of the population. Cihangir was in the 19th century – under the influence of westernization – the housing area of part of the western-oriented minority groups, Jews and Armenians, in late Ottoman times, with four- and five-storey, massive apartment houses (UZUN 2003, p. 368). In Kuzguncuk, where Jews, Greeks and Armenians lived beside the Muslim population, the old type of wooden houses existed (UZUN, 2003, pp. 369–370).

After the foundation of the state of Israel in 1948 many Jews left; Armenians had moved out already in and after the First World War; Greeks of Istanbul emigrated from the city after reprisals in 1955. So both areas were prepared for the invasion of a new population that could afford the renovation and modernization of the old stone-houses in Cihangir and wooden houses in Kuzguncuk. In Cihangir artists, academics and writers moved in. The Turkish winner of the Nobel Prize for literature, ORHAN PAMUK, grew up, lives and works there (STEWIG 2006). He organizes a museum in the area, referring to his literary work (Museum of Innocence in Çukurcuma).

In Kuzguncuk, where art collectors live, an individual, the architect-author Cengiz Bektaş initiated the gentrification of the area with the strict aim of protecting an ancient urban environment (UZUN 2003, p. 369).

In both cases the up-grading was not primarily a question of economics – though the new occupants had to pay for the revalorization – but to a great extent a matter of culture. It is not unusual that World Cities have their own artists' quarters.

e   *Urbanization of Istanbul Province*

Even the strictly economistically oriented World City researchers admit that population is important in connection with World Cities. The example of high-ranking financial off-shore centres which are no World Cities is sufficiently illustrative.

The number of inhabitants is important for the evaluation of Istanbul as a World City – in the past and in modern times, though with different scales for ranking.

The development of Istanbul is the story of its population growth caused by continued domestic migration from rural areas – and in modern times – small urban settlements, a migration which fits-in with push- und pull-forces in the two different areas of origin and destination (YERASIMOS 1997).

In 1950 the percentage of people living in the province of Istanbul but were born outside was as low as 47% (YERASIMOS 1997, p. 199). In 1980 the percentage amounted to 61,78, in 1985 to 61,03, in 1990 to 62,73 and in 2000 to 62, 24 (Devlet Istatistik Enstitüsü 2002, p. 44). This means that migration to Istanbul continued on a steady high level.

It is a general rule of the formation of World Cities – observed for the first time in London in the 19th century – that a suburbanization process begins. This means that people residing in the inner city move to the periphery. But when great masses of people migrate to a large city they also settle – from the beginning – in the periphery.

This was the case in Istanbul in the period of gecekondus, beginning slowly in the 1950s (TÜMERTEKIN 1970/1971; YERASIMOS 1997, pp. 196–206).

At first a nearly closed ring of gecekondu settlements formed itself outside the old city quarters beyond the Great Land Wall and the Golden Horn, in Zeytinburnu (123 000), Bayrampaşa (157 000), Gaziosmanpaşa (162 000), Alibeyköy (33 000), Kağıthane (164 000), Esenler (49 000), Güngören (49 000) about 1975 (YERASIMOS 1997, p. 206).

With uninterrupted, even increased migration to Istanbul since the 1980s a second, quasi-ring, farther outside, formed itself, largely unplanned. This means that the built-up area of Istanbul expanded into agriculturally used parts of the province of Istanbul. And this means that the rate of urbanization of the province of Istanbul boosted from 61,3 % in 1980 to 92,4 % in 1990 and 90,6 % in 2000 (Devlet Istatistik Enstitüsü 2002, p. 42).

The increase of urban districts (ilce) within the province of Istanbul mirrors the process of (sub-) urbanization. In 1980 19 districts existed, in 1990 25, in 2000 32 (Devlet Istatistik Enstitüsü 2002, p. 61). Lately the number was increased to 39 (ESEN, RIENIETS 2008, p. 100-footnote). A comparison of the number of inhabitants of the 32 districts of the province of Istanbul in 1990 and in 2000 will reveal the enormous increase in the outermost districts, the emergence of a second quasi-ring of (sub)urbanization.

Districts of the Province of Istanbul	1990	2000
Adalar (islands)	19 413	17 760
Avcılar	126 493	233 749
Bağcılar	291 457	556 519

Bahçelievler	298 211	478 623
Bakırköy	301 673	308 398
Bayrampaşa	212 570	246 006
Beşiktaş	192 210	19 813
Beykoz	161 609	210 832
Beyoğlu	229 000	231 900
Eminönü	83 444	55 635
Esenler	223 826	380 709
Eyüp	211 986	255 912
Fatih	462 464	403 508
Gaziosmanpaşa	393 667	752 389
Güngören	213 109	272 950
Kadıköy	648 282	663 299
Kağıthane	269 045	345 239
Kartal	273 572	407 865
Küçükçekmece	352 926	594 524
Maltepe	245 256	355 384
Pendik	200 907	389 657
Sariyer	171 872	242 543
Şişli	250 478	270 674
Tuzla	96 150	123 255
Ümraniye	308 434	605 855
Üsküdar	395 623	495 118
Büyükçekmece	142 910	384 089
Çatalca	64 241	81 589
Sultanbeyli	82 298	175 700
Şile	25 372	32 447

(Devlet Istatistik Enstitüsü 2002, p. 61).

The table proves the existence in Istanbul (province and city) of two counter developments typical of very large (and even smaller) cities: reduction of population or stagnant population in the innermost administrative districts and exceptionally high rates of population increase in the outer districts of Avcılar, Bağcılar, Bahçelievler, Esenler, Gaziosmanpaşa, Kartal, Küçükçekmece, Maltepe, Pendik, Ümraniye, Büyükçekmece. These processes are effective on both, the western and the eastern sides of the Bosphorus. No wonder that the total number of inhabitants of Istanbul has been and still is rapidly growing.

Turkish statistics distinguish between rural and urban districts within provinces.

Since 1980 the number of population of the province of Istanbul increased from 4 741 890 (1980) to 7 309 190 in 1990 and to 10 018 735 in 2000 (Devlet Istatistik Enstitüsü 2002, p. 42). The administrative districts classed as urban amounted to 2 909 455 in 1980, to 6 753 929 in 1990 and to 9 085 599 in 2000 (Devlet Istatistik Enstitüsü 2002, p. 42).

There is a varying degree of population in rural administrative districts of the province of Istanbul: 1 832 435 in 1980, 555 261 in 1990 and 933 136 in 2000, but this has to do with changes of the boundaries of the districts.

If the class of Mega Cities begins with a population of 10 million and more Istanbul was already in 2000 on the verge of a Mega City. With 9.3 million in 2000 listed by SCOTT (2001/2008, p. 3-table) this would mean rank 23 of the world's thirty largest urban areas – no doubt, sufficient to class Istanbul as a World City on the basis of population alone. The projection for 2050 is 16 million and rank 19 (BRUNN, HAYS-MITCHELL, ZEIGLER 2008, p. 567-table) with a decreasing rate of growth: from 3,94 % as the annual rate of change in the 1975–1995 period to 3,22 % in the 1995–2015 period (STREN 2001/2008, p. 199-table).

f   *World City Retail Infrastructure*

Normally the provisioning of urban population with commodities of life – food, clothing and many other things – is nothing special that qualifies a large city as a World City. But there are different levels of supply, mainly between large and small cities, which is not a question of quantity alone, and between cities in developed and in developing countries.

From the 1980s onwards Istanbul (TOKATLI, BOYACIA 1998, 1999; TIMOR 2004; STEWIG 2009) – almost all of a sudden – experienced spectacular changes in the structure and quality of its retail system. This has to do with the new economic policy in Turkey since 1980.

Before that time, in the Ottoman period, Istanbul showed the retail structure and quality which was typical of large cities in developing countries: the bazaar, south of the Golden Horn, as the dominating retail (and wholesale and banking) centre together with the numerous small retail centres in the many city quarters; besides street vendors, corner shops and weekly open markets existed.

Under the influence of westernization in the 19th century a new centre developed north of the Golden Horn, the Grande Rue de Pera, the area of the westernized part of Istanbul.

This meant that there was a first aggravating change of the retail system, an innovation, an addition to the traditional structure which continued to exist – though there were some other changes before 1980 when the Swiss firm Migros introduced the first supermarkets in Istanbul (TOKATLI, BOYACI 19989, p. 346). Traditional open markets continued to exist in great numbers (ÖZGÜÇ, MITCHELL 2000; SEGER, PALENCSAR 2006, p. 138-map).

Then, in 1988 the first American-type, mall-type shopping-centre, the "Galleria", was founded (TIMOR 2004; STEWIG 2009). This did not remain an exception. In 2010 about 50 modern-type shopping-centres existed, distributed over large parts of Istanbul, in a western and a northern axis on the Thracian side of the Bosphorus and a little more dispersed on the Anatolian side of Istanbul (TOKATLI, BOYACI 1999, p. 189; TIMOR 2004; STEWIG 2009, pp. 59–65-maps).

Several types may be distinguished: a first wave of shopping-centres, some now closed because of competiton of later and larger ones. There are – mostly in the inner city areas – tower buildings with many storeys either above ground (Cevahir, Astoria) or even below ground (MetroCity). In the periphery is more space for expansion, so a new development may be observed which perhaps will turn out as the forerunner of a new pattern, even outside Istanbul, the evolution of retail-complexes consisting not only of mall-type shopping centres – even several – but also – additionally – of one or two hypermarkets and special centres like IKEA (for furniture) or BAUHAUS (building material for amateurs) or Media Markt (electronic IT equipment) (STEWIG 2009).

Clearly, foreign retail firms, globally operating, have invaded Istanbul, sometimes in co-operation as joint-ventures, sometimes in partly possession of large domestic holding companies, conglomerates, like Sabancı Holding, Koç Holding, Tekfen Holding (TOKATLI, BOYACI 1998, p. 348).

The customers are at least middle class urbanites with sufficient income to own a private car. So shopping-centres and shopping-centre-complexes have to care for parking space. In the inner city area they do this by underground parking space, in the periphery large parking space on level ground evokes the typical impression observers are acquainted with from American and other large cities.

This retail structure can be classified as normal in the city of Istanbul. As for the quality, specially of the mall-type shopping-centres, their shops offer international labels of life-style.

A new trend is also impressive: the combination with gastronomy and entertainments, in one case ("Galleria") even with an ice-skating platform. Also events are more or less regularly staged to promote shopping. In some shopping-centres extravagant architecture does more than necessary.

With this structure and quality of the retail system Istanbul need not hide behind other World Cities.

g World City Traffic Infrastructure

The notion of infrastructure refers first of all to the inner urban situation (LEITNER 1965, 1967; MÜLLER-WIENER 1994; STEWIG 1964, 2006).

But, Istanbul having been classed as an at least partly global financial centre, the question has to be asked, if there are appropriate international traffic connections. It has to be admitted that there are deficiencies.

When air traffic originated and increased internationally after the Second World War – at a time when Istanbul was in a period of decline – it passed the city almost completely (STEWIG 1964, p. 65-map), although in 1953 a modern airport was inaugurated, the Atatürk airport, on the western fringe of the city (ROTHFISCHER 2007, p. 92). Even the economic boom since the 1980s as an effect of the new economic policy did not cause a massive change of the situation immediately. There are long distance flight connections (SEGER, PALENCSAR 2006, p. 42-map). Things are improving. In 2006 Atatürk Airport scored rank 47 among 100 airports with 23 261 878 passengers (ROTHFISCHER 2007, p. 287-table). In 2009 the Atatürk Airport had reached rank 39 of 100 airports with 29 854 119 passengers (Aero 9, 2010, p. 27-table). Since 2002 Atatürk Airport has a rail connection to the central city.

A second airport, Sabiha Gökçen, on the Anatolian side, named after the adopted daughter of Atatürk and first female pilot in Turkey, was opened in 2002.

The major air routes are destined to the neighbouring countries in Europe, Central Asia and the Middle East. The share of international passengers was 61,6% in 2009, which placed the Atatürk Airport on rank 20 among the 25 largest airports according to international passengers (Aero, 9, 2010, p. 29-table). But the passengers are not in the first line businessmen, but tourists and people of Turkish origin living in Europe. The fastest growing airport on the globe is the Sabiha Gökçen Airport (Aero, 9, 2010, p. 30-table) with 52,3% passenger increase 2009.

As for Istanbul's function in connection with long distance shipping traffic of goods – unimportant for the inner urban infrastructure – there existed for a long time – since the opening of the Suez Canal in 1869 (STEWIG 1964,

p. 55-map) – an underdeveloped situation. The Bosphorus – as a watery passage a whim of nature – with heavy shipping traffic of bulk cargo (grain, oil) from the Black Sea is an important sea lane running through the middle of a World City, but with little economic effect to the city (STEWIG 1964, pp. 52–61; 2006).

As far as the inner urban traffic structure of Istanbul is concerned the situation is today not too far away from the level of World Cities. And this situation began already before 1980.

The period of westernization in the 19th century brought a short underground rack-railway in 1874 to the city, of course, to the westernized area north of the Golden Horn (STEWIG 2006, p. 609). Tramways, the first horse drawn, later with electric engines, were also introduced (GÜLERSOY 1989). Long distance railways – originally intended for international passenger transport – the Orient-Express Paris-Istanbul in 1873 and the Anatolian and Baghdad Railway in 1888 – came to be used, in the long run, for inner urban, suburban traffic. These are infrastructural components comparable with other large cities of the time.

Further improvements of the inner urban traffic situation also started before the 1980s: the construction of the first Bosphorus bridge in 1973 on occasion of the 50th anniversary of the Turkish Republic. It was urgently needed: the Bosphorus ferries were unable to cope much longer with the inner urban traffic between the eastern and the western half of Istanbul across the Bosphorus.

It was high time for further improvements, because the transformation of the traditional, pre-industrial, pedestrian city to an automobile city with a large share of private cars had already begun (STEWIG 2006).

An elaborate system of inner urban motorways was devised and implemented together with a second Bosphorus bridge in 1988 (STEWIG 2006, p. 264-map). With the inner urban motorways as a system Istanbul can today compete with other World Cities: two parallel super-highways across the Bosphorus and several connecting links exist.

Inner urban rail transport is still showing deficiencies though endeavours to remedy the situation are under way (STEWIG 2006, p. 265-map). Particularly links between the separate lines are lacking.

There is a suburban light railway (hafif metro) on the western half of Istanbul south of the Golden Horn which is – since 2002 – connecting the Atatürk Airport with the central city. And there is – since 2000 – a new, underground railway (metro) leading north of the Golden Horn from the Taksim Square to the new business centre in northern Istanbul.

The expansion of the existing rail connections and their linkage are urgently desired and planned. Especially on the Anatolian side of Istanbul, presently in vivid transformation from a purely residential to a partly business area, rail connections are much in want (STEWIG 2006, p. 256-map). The new international airport, the Sabiha Gökçen Airport, in tremendous growth, has no rail connection.

A future highlight of infrastructural improvements is coming shortly: the opening of the Bosphorus railway tunnel will bring a rapid rail connection between Sirkeci, the main railway station of the old quarters of the city of Istanbul, west of the Bosphorus, and Üsküdar, respectively Haydarpaşa, originally Istanbul's railway station for long distance travel will serve primarily inner urban requirements. There have been dreams of a new Silk Road on rails (STEWIG 2006, p. 112; HÜBNER, KAMLAH, REINFANDT 2001).

As far as traffic infrastructure is concerned Istanbul fulfils only partly the standards of a World City.

b   Istanbul as a Manufacturing City

The first questions to be asked are: what has manufacturing to do with World Cities and what is Istanbul's position in this connection (TÜMERTEKIN 1961, 1970/71, 1972; STEWIG 1964, pp. 66–68; LEITNER 1969, 1971; ÖZGÜÇ 1986, 1986/87; STANDL 1994; BAZIN, DE TAPIA 1999). Even if the answers – as may be anticipated – are negative, the holistic approach to World Cities demands consideration of these aspects.

Modern manufacturing, i.e. production with the use of machines, started in Istanbul in the period of modernization of the Ottoman Empire in the 19th century. Comparatively large plants were opened by the state for the supply of the Ottoman army with headgear (fez), uniforms and shoes, for which cloth mills and leather factories were located on the upper Golden Horn and in Beykoz on the Bosphorus (CLARK 1974; STANDL 1994).

Tobacco processing (Orient cigarettes) was also important, part of the products were exported.

As the largest consumer agglomeration of the Ottoman Empire, later of Turkey, there were plenty of chances for privately owned, small, artisanal-like manufacturing shops in Istanbul.

After the First World War the city did not only loose the function of political capital of Turkey, but its manufacturing capacity was curtailed by the new government's industrialization endeavours outside Istanbul.

In 1950 Istanbul had only 36 manufacturing plants with more than 200 workers (TÜMERTEKIN 1961, p. 43). On the whole Istanbul accounted for about 25 % of the industrial activities of Turkey then (TÜMERTEKIN 1961, p. 43). There were great differences between various branches (STEWIG 1964, p. 67-table), but consumer oriented production prevailed.

Before 1980 the import-substitution policy of economic activities in Istanbul and Turkey reigned, bringing a wave of privately owned manufacturing shops to the city.

The share of Istanbul of Turkish industry amounted in 1964 to 42,9 %, in 1982 to 47,4 % (establishments), in 1964 to 36 %, in 1982 to 32,5 % (workers), in 1964 to 38,5 % and in 1982 to 32 % (value added) (ÖZGÜÇ 1986, p. 59-table, 1986/1987, p. 54-table). The cities of Izmir and Ankara were far below Istanbul's share at about 4 to 7 % in all three sections.

This means that Istanbul, though having lost the title of political capital, acquired – additionally – to its function as business capital the title of industrial capital.

The new economic policy of the 1980s increased Istanbul's primacy as the foremost manufacturing city of Turkey. In this period export was not only promoted, but actually subsidized. Ready-made goods were exported to developed countries in Europe and elsewhere: textiles (jeans) and durable consumer goods like washing machines, refrigerators, television sets. Joint-ventures, combinations of Turkish holding companies with foreign, globally operating firms (BAZIN, DE TAPIA 1999, p. 125) created an automobile assembly industry, which settled in Istanbul and outside (for example in Bursa) to supply the home market, even before the 1980s.

There was a new inner urban arrangement of localization: plants settled along highways, very much so on the Anatolian side of Istanbul (STANDL 1994), and in planned industrial parks: Ikitelli on the Thracian side of Istanbul being one of the best known (STANDL 1994, pp. 78–82).

The old industrial locations on the Golden Horn were given up (HELLER, GERDES 1991).

Presently a process of industrialization has begun outside Istanbul, in many parts of the country (BAZIN, DE TAPIA 1999). This diminishes a little the position of Istanbul, but the city is as much as in the past the unimpeached master of manufacturing in Turkey.

However, this position is not a contribution to Istanbul as a World city, at least not a direct one. Indirectly the very strong manufacturing position of Istanbul in Turkey draws many migrants to the city who in turn increase the population. At least part of the industrial workforce of Istanbul strengthens the World City rank on the basis of numbers of inhabitants.

Additionally Istanbul is the dominant location of the headquarters of Turkish holding companies, conglomerates with global connections, which own large parts of manufacturing companies in Turkey (BUĞRA 1994, pp. 57, 181–224).

i Istanbul as a Capital of Culture

A reminder first, the research of World Cities, practiced by economists and sociologists, is here enlarged to a holistic approach which includes the aspect of culture (STEWIG 1986; LEITNER 1989; DÖKMECI, BALTA 1999; STOKES 1999; SOMER 2005; DÖKMECI, ALTUNBAŞ, YAZGI 2007); (HANNERZ 1992, 1996; SCOTT 1997; KING 2007).

Admittedly there are sociologists who have recognized the importance of culture in connection with and as part of World Cities (SASSEN 2006, pp. 160–161).

It has already been explained in the publication that – according to the ideas of the German philopher Wilhelm Dilthey (1833–1911) – culture appears in almost every field of life. Here culture is of interest with World Cities and with what has been called the "cultural economy of cities" (SCOTT 1997), which is important. In his essay SCOTT even considers the production of everyday commodities as part of the cultural economy of cities. This is a digression which will not be taken up.

The following fields of culture are distinguished in connection with Istanbul as a capital of culture: artistic culture, culture of events, culture for tourists, night-life culture.

α Artistic Culture

In this group artistic utterances are in the middle of consideration, static and dynamic presentations of music (classic and popular), painting, sculpture, dance/ballet, theatre, film, perhaps also fashion and design. As long as the presentations do not rely on knowledge of the Turkish language – which is limited in an international context – the range of attraction is theoretically wide, depending on the reputation of artefacts, institutions, museums.

In connection with the award of the title of European Capital of Culture to Istanbul in 2010, great pains have been taken in the city – privately and from the municipality – to enlarge and improve attractiveness. The list of museums in Istanbul is to be found in city-guide books (GORYS 2003, pp. 211–213). The newest and most spectacular museums are the Museum of Modern Art in the port area north of the Golden Horn, in a former customs depot, the Santral

Istanbul, a museum as an arts centre in a former ancient electricity power station on the Golden Horn, the Hasanpaşa Gasworks as a cultural centre, preserving the industrial legacy of Istanbul on the Anatolian side.

As a category of its own there is – opened in 2009 – the spectacular Panorama 1453-Museum, re-enacting in a grand manner, with sound and a gigantic all-round painting/mural, the conquest of Constantinople in 1453.

There is an astonishingly large number of small art galleries in the city (SOMER 2005, pp. 328–332), 119 in all, 3 state-owned, 12 belonging to the municipality, 104 private ones. This is primarily of local interest, not a contribution to Istanbul as a World City.

β Culture of Events

An impressive culture of events, ranging from arts via sports to politics, is staged in Istanbul, some of them with international reputation.

The best known annual festivals are (– this is a selection from a list already rendered):
– International Film Festival
– International Theatre Festival
– International Music Festival
– International Jazz Festival
– International Biennial of Visual Arts (GORYS 2003, p. 210).

Besides, there are 14 others, more or less international, more or less annual festivals in Istanbul. The Grand Prix d'Eurovision/European Song Contest took place in Istanbul in 2004.

Of sporting events – besides international football championships – the annual Formula One racing event since 2005 is a first rank highlight. The city has – unsuccessfully – applied for staging the Olympic Games in Istanbul, a stadium already constructed.

Istanbul is an internationally favourite place for political and economic conferences/conventions.

The Second United Nations Human Settlement Conference (Habitat II) met in Istanbul in 1996. The International Monetary Fund (IMF) and the World Bank hold meetings in Istanbul. The International World Water Forum convened in Istanbul in 2009. The Organization of Islamic States met for the 2009 conference in Istanbul. In 2010 Afghanistan was the subject of the conference of defence ministers of armed forces engaged in that country. The International Somalia Conference about piracy was held in Istanbul in 2010. The third Global

Economic Symposium with 500 participating scientists took place in Istanbul in September 2010. A number of minor events will not be listed here.

γ Culture for Tourists
Of great importance for a city – and especially for a World City – is what may be called cultural tourism (STEINECKE 2007).

Two types of tourists have to be distinguished, native tourists of Istanbul (STEWIG 1986) and foreign tourists who arrive either by plane or by ship (cruise liners). They have to be accommodated in hotels and this is an important economic task of the city (DÖKMECI, BALTA 1999). Of course, hotels also serve the participants of festivals, conferences and other events.

The number of tourists increased tremendously in Istanbul from 71 227 in 1960 to 1 121 931 in 1990. The absolute increase ran parallel with a decrease of Istanbul's share of tourists in Turkey from 57,3 % in 1960 to 20,8 % in 1990 (DÖKMECI, BALTA 1999, p. 100-table), due to the promotion of tourism in Turkey outside Istanbul.

The development of tourism in Istanbul caused an appropriate development of hotels.

When the western style of accommodating travellers in hotels was introduced in Istanbul in the period of westernization in the 19th century, the first hotel, the Hotel d'Angleterre, opened in 1841, north of the Golden Horn, in the westernized area of Istanbul (DÖKMECI, BALTA 1999, p. 101). The Orient-Express from Paris to Istanbul brought more tourists to Istanbul. In 1892 the famous Pera Palace Hotel – still in operation – was organized by the Wagons-Lits Company; it derives its reputation from Agatha Christie, once a guest.

In 1938 22 hotels existed in Istanbul, 269 in Turkey (DÖKMECI, BALTA 1999, p. 101). The first modern hotel, the Hilton, was opened in 1955 as a joint-venture of Turkish and foreign capital (DÖKMECI, BALTA 1999, p. 101).

Since the 1980s there was a further marked increase of hotels (and tourism) in Istanbul. In 2005 29 five-star hotels existed in the city, 28 on the western side of the Bosphorus, one on the Anatolian side; 73 four-star hotels, 72 on the western side, one on the Anatolian side; 46 three-star hotels, 40 on the western side of the Bosphorus, 6 on the Anatolian side. Of 230 listed hotels 211 are to be found west of the Bosphorus, 19 east of the Bosphorus (SOMER 2005, pp. 228–259). This precarious disequilibrium is illustrative of the spatial differences within the city of Istanbul: touristic attractions are almost all on the Thracian side, the area which is usually called the European side.

The mass of first rank hotels in Istanbul, many of them hotel towers, is located in a relatively confined area north of the Taksim Square, at the northern end of the İstiklal Caddesi, the former Grande Rue de Pera.

The foreign tourists – and this is the general attitude of city tourists (HANNERZ 1996 in BRENNER, KEIL, p. 318) – hasten from one highlight to the next. This is in Istanbul the Aya Sofya/St. Sophia, standing for the Christian past, the Topkapı Sarayı/Seraglio Palace, the Sultan Ahmet-mosque and the Dolmabahçe Palace, standing for the Ottoman past. Stereotypes of traditional Oriental life-style are also requested: the bazaar, belly dance, Whirling Dervishes, bath-houses, Turkish cuisine.

Since the dissolution of the Soviet Block a new type of tourist appears regularly in Istanbul and in numbers, from the newly independent neighbouring states west, north and east of the Black Sea, for purchasing textile and leather goods in a city-quarter (Laleli) on the western edge of the bazaar (PALENCSAR, KREIS 2000). For these people, staying in Istanbul for two or three nights, hotels of lower level developed.

The connection between high-ranking events, distinguished tourism and super-class hotels and hotel-chains of international reputation is obvious in Istanbul and demonstrates the World City status in this respect.

δ Night-life Culture

This type of culture should not be underestimated in large cities in general and in Istanbul in particular (cp. SASSEN 2006, p. 161): night-life culture (GORYS 2003, pp. 203–205).

Not only tourists but also the high-income population of Istanbul, businessmen, yuppies (young urban professionals) and others, indulge in the attractions of night-life.

This is located in Istanbul in and around the İstiklal Caddesi, the ancient Grande Rue de Pera, an area where the old western apartment houses with large rooms and four to five storeys, dating from the 19th century, stand.

Originally the noble main street of Beyoğlu, the old Pera and Galata region, decayed when Istanbul lost its function as political capital (DÖKMECI, ALTUNBAŞ, YAZGI 2007). But since the 1980s the street and its surroundings experienced a miraculous revitalization as an entertainment centre ranging from literary clubs via restaurants, bars, today also fast-food shops, to meeting-places of gays and lesbians (GORYS 2003, pp. 202–205) – exceptional for an Islamic country. Street life is part of its attraction (PREHL 2008).

The revival was initiated by the change of the street into a pedestrian walkway, with installation of an old-time tram in 1990 (DÖKMECI, ALTUNBAŞ, YAZGI 2007).

For the removal of car traffic a broad highway was constructed in Tarlabaşı, parallel to the old main street, for which a lot of houses were demolished which created sorrow and protest from the architectural side (Architektenkammer Istanbul 1989, pp. 1740–1741).

For many countries in the surroundings of Turkey, where Islam is practised in a stricter way than in Turkey, the night-life culture of Istanbul is an attraction and has a catchment area far beyond Turkey's borders.

As a summarizing evaluation it is justified to state that of the many facets of culture in Istanbul several can be classed as of World City rank, particularly those for which the language barrier is not a hindrance.

This applies partly to education as part of culture: Istanbul is the primary city for university education in Turkey, though Ankara is runner-up (LEITNER 1989).

It is true, in most of the universities of Istanbul (FREY 1968/1070; WIDMANN 1985; LEITNER 1989; SOMER 2005, pp. 384–395) the language is Turkish. But the situation is different in those universities organized by private enterprise, in the past and recently. There are the historical colleges, today classed as universities, founded by French and American initiatives in the 19th century (formerly Galata Sarayı and Robert College). And there are private universities, founded by Turkish industrialists and holding companies (Koç, Sabancı) in the recent past where English is the common means of communication. This makes these universities attractive beyond Turkey, for neighbouring countries.

j   Evaluation

Before the 1980s Istanbul was still suffering from the loss of the function of political capital, was the melancholy city PAMUK (2003) had painted in his novel/documentary about Istanbul in his youth. The more it is amazing and surprising that and how a fundamental change of economic policy in Turkey improved the situation of the country's largest city and fostered its development to World City rank.

Recent World City research has overcome the old paradigm of monographic and idiographic delineations, but has – in a one-sided way – stressed the economic (FRIEDMANN 1986) and sociologic (SASSEN 2006) aspects. This has been respected in connection with World City research about Istanbul, but the new paradigm has been expanded to a holistic approach. The result is a greater number of criteria for World City rank.

As a minor global financial centre Istanbul has attained World City status. It has been recognized that in conjunction with this rank high-income and low-income migrants, domestic migrants and foreigners, moved and still move to the city, which is leading to social polarization, described by sociologists (SASSEN 2006) investigating World Cities elsewhere.

In this connection – in the case of Istanbul as elsewhere – several criteria are indicative of the social situation: the existence of mass housing in Istanbul (relatively comfortable high-rise apartment towers) in the periphery of the city; the existence of gated communities, in the periphery in horizontal compounds, in the city in vertical apartment towers; the existence of gentrification – in Istanbul for artists' quarters – and revitalization of inner city areas.

Aspects generally neglected by the advocates of the new paradigm of World City research but dealt with for Istanbul – is the existence of a most modern retail structure based on mall-type shopping centres, and the existence of a comprehensive modern inner urban traffic infrastructure, in Istanbul based more on motorways than on rail connections. Admittedly some inner urban regions of Istanbul are still in want of a systematic inner urban rail pattern, particularly the Anatolian side.

The number of inhabitants in a sizable measure is meanwhile recognized by the new World Research paradigm as an important criterion for World City rank and applies fully to Istanbul.

There is another field of society, underestimated so far by World City researchers of the new school: this is the wide realm of culture. However, it is increasingly and generally acknowledged that the culture of cities is a constituent element of World Cities. This reasonable view confirms the necessity of a holistic approach. In this matter Istanbul does not belong to the first rank of cultural World Cities, but has to offer several outstanding performances.

As a summary statement: Istanbul's rise to World City rank since the 1980s was on the whole successful, though Istanbul cannot compete with the top ranks of World Cities.

D. Istanbul's Identity

At the beginning of this publication it was clearly stated that three aspects will be followed. The first is the question if Istanbul can rightly by called a European Capital of Culture as the title awarded for 2010 implies.

The second question deals with Istanbul as a possible World City/Global City/Mega City.

The third aspect is the combination of the first two, the problem of Istanbul's identity.

All aspects are an approach on the basis of a holistic conception.

The answer to the first question is that Istanbul – the full length of its history is included – is a hybrid, the meeting place of impacts from distant lands, societies, cultures.

The Christian, European, Greek and Roman influences prevailed for a very long time when Constantinople was the political and religious capital of the Byzantine Empire. The situation changed when a new population of Central Asian origin, speaking Turkish, took over. Combined with the population was its divine creed, the Oriental religion of Islam, at home in Arabic lands. Another impact, a cosmopolitan one, came from Western lands with new life-styles, the development of different demographic and social structures and the adoption of modern technology and politics.

With these components Istanbul may well be called – as has been done – a crossroads city.

The World City aspect is not less important for Istanbul's identity. It is exceptional that the city attained three times in the course of history World City rank.

For the first time this happened as the political, religious and commercial capital of the Byzantine Empire with a wide range of competence for parts of the Old World.

For the second time this happened as the political, in a way religious and partly commercial capital city of the Ottoman Empire with again its competence in parts of the Old World.

For the third time Istanbul attained minor World City rank as the economic and cultural capital city of Turkey with global connections.

In each case it is remarkable that Constantinople and Istanbul were and are outstanding cities of endogenous culture, in Byzantine and Ottoman times as capitals of culture for a wide territory, in late Ottoman and Republican times as representations of cosmopolitan culture with a limited range of influence.

The rise to World City rank three times in the history of Constantinople – Istanbul is embedded in societal evolution. During the first two times the structure of the city shared the common traits of large urban settlements of medieval agrarian society. Between the second and the third achievement of World City rank the transformation of society set in massively. At the present Istanbul's structure as a World City shows the typical traits of large urban places of industrial societies.

Of the many features of change the transformation of the inner urban traffic structure is the most illustrative one: it is the evolution from the pedestrian city of pre-industrial society to the automobile city of advanced industrial society.

If a short verbal formula is requested: Istanbul is a crossroads economic and cultural World City, over long periods also a political capital, with a rich culture of Byzantine churches and Ottoman mosques, on – in contrast to several regions in Turkey – the level of industrial society.

E. Publications

ABU-LUGHOD, J.L. (1989): Before European Hegemony: The World System A.D. 1250–1350. New York, Oxford.

ADORNO, T.W. (1991): The Culture Industry. Selected Essays on Mass Culture. London.

AKSOY, A. (2008): Istanbul's Worldliness; in: ECKARDT, F., WILDNER, K. (eds.): Public Istanbul. Spaces and Spheres of the Urban. Bielefeld, pp. 215–232.

ALKAN, S. (2008): Globalization and the Struggle over a Living Space. The Case of Karanfilköy; in: ECKARDT, F., WILDNER, K. (eds.): Public Istanbul. Spaces and Spheres of the Urban. Bielefeld, pp. 49–81.

AMELUNG, T. (1989): Die politische Ökonomie der Importsubstitution and der Handelsliberalisierung. Das Beispiel Türkei. Kieler Studien 227. Tübingen.

Architektenkammer Istanbul (1988): Totenklage für Tarlabaşı; in: Bauwelt 79, 40. Berlin, pp. 1740–1741.

ARIN, C. (1988): Adieu Istanbul. Agonie einer Weltstadt? In: Bauwelt 49, 40. Berlin, pp. 1736–1737.

AYATAC, H., DÖKMECI, V. (2007): Spatial Analysis of Library System and Proposal for New Libraries in Istanbul; in: European Planning Studies 15, 3. Oxford, New York, pp. 1127–1137.

BABINGER, F. (1961): Die Donau als Schicksalsstrom des Osmanischen Reiches; in: Südosteuropa-Jahrbuch 5. München, pp. 15–27.

BACHTELER, K. (ed.) (1969): Istanbul. Beiträge zur Geschichte und Entwicklung der Stadt am Goldenen Horn. Ludwigsburg (Series: Karawane-Taschenbuch).

BÄHR, J. (1993): Verstädterung der Erde; in: Geographische Rundschau 45. Braunschweig, pp. 468–472.

BÄHR, J., JÜRGENS, U. (2005): Stadtgeographie II. Regionale Stadtgeographie. Braunschweig (Series: Das Geographische Seminar).

BATUR, A. (ed.) (1996): Dünya Kenti Istanbul. Istanbul – World City. Istanbul.

BAZIN, M. (ed.) (2009): Le Caire, Istanbul, Teheran. Les trois métropoles du Moyen Orient. Travaux de l'Institut de Géographie de Reims 127/128. Reims.

BAZIN, M., DE TAPIA, S. (1999): L'industrialisation de la Turquie: processus de développement et dynamiques spatiales; in: Mediterrané 3/4. Aix-en-Provence, pp. 121–133.

BEAVERSTOCK, J.V., TAYLOR, P.J., SMITH, R.G. (1999): A Roster of World Cities; in: Cities 16. Oxford, pp. 445–458.

BENGTSON, H. (1960): Griechische Geschichte von den Anfängen bis in die Römische Kaiserzeit. Handbuch der Altertumswissenschaft. 3rd ed. München.

BERKÖZ, L. (1998): Locational Preferences of Producer Firms in Istanbul; in: European Planning Studies 6,3. Oxford, New York, pp. 333–349.

BERKÖZ, L. (2000): Location of Financial, Insurance and Real Estate Firms in Istanbul; in: Journal of Urban Planning and Development 126, 2. Reston, Va., pp. 75–88.

BERKÖZ, L., EYUBOĞLU, E. (2007): Intrametropolitan Location of Producerservices FDI in Istanbul; in: European Planning Studies 15, 3. Oxford, New York, pp. 357–381.

BOULANGER, R., CASE, M (1961): Istanbul and Environs. Paris (Series: Hachette World Guides).

BRANDS, H.W. (1974): Die Sprache; in: KÜNDIG-STEINER, R.W. (ed.): Die Türkei. Raum und Mensch, Kultur und Wirtchaft in Gegenwart und Vergangenheit. Tübingen, Basel, pp. 198–201. (Series: Ländermonograpahien 4. Institut für Auslandsbeziehungen, Stuttgart).

BRAUDEL, F. (1986): Sozialgeschichte des 15. –18. Jahrhunderts. Aufbruch zur Weltwirtschaft. München.

BRENNER, N., KEIL, R. (eds.) (2006): The Global Cities Reader. London, New York.

BRONGER, D. (1984): Metropolisierung als Entwicklungsproblem in den Ländern der Dritten Welt. Ein Beitrag zur Begriffsbestimmung; in: Geographische Zeitschrift 72. Stuttgart, pp. 138–158.

BRONGER, D. (2004): Metropolen, Megastädte, Global Cities. Die Metropolisierung der Erde. Darmstadt.

BRUNS, S.D., WILLIAMS, J.F. (1993): Cities of the World. World Regional Urban Development. 2nd ed. New York.

BRUNN, S., HAYS-MITCHELL, M., ZEIGLER, D.J. (eds.) (2008): Cities of the World. World Regional Urban Development. 4th ed. Lanham, Boulder, New York, Toronto, Plymouth U.K.

BUĞRA, A. (1994): State and Business in Modern Turkey. A Comparative Study. New York.

CASTELLS, M. (1989): The Informational City. Information, Technology, Economic Restructuring and the Urban Regional Process. Oxford.

CASTELLS, M. (1993): European Cities, the Informational Society and the Global Economy; in: Tijdschrift voor Economische en Sociale Geografie 84, 4. Oxford, pp. 247–257.

CHANDLER, T., FOX, G. (1974): Three Thousand Years of Urban Growth. New York.

CHASE-DUNN, C.K. (1985): The System of World Cities, A.D. 800–9175; in: TIMBERLAKE, M. (ed): Urbanisation in the World Economy. Orlando, San Diego, New York, London, Toronto, Montreal, Sidney, Tokyo, pp. 269–292.

CHAVARDÉS, M., CHAVARDÉS, M. (1963): La Chute de Constantinople 29 mai 1453. Paris.

CLARK, E.C. (1974): The Ottoman Industrial Revolution; in: International Journal of Middle East Studies 5. Cambridge, pp. 65–76.

DANIELSON, M.N., KELEŞ, R. (1985): The Politics of Rapid Urbanization. Government and Growth in Modern Turkey. New York, London.

DAVISON, H. (1963): Reform in the Ottoman Empire 1856–1876. Princeton, N.J.

Devlet Istatistik Enstitüsü/State Institute of Statistics (2002): Türkiye Istatistik Yıllığı 2001. Statistical Yearbook of Turkey. Ankara.

Devlet Istatistik Enstitüsü/State Institute of Statistics (2202): Il/Province. 34 – Istanbul. 2000 Genel Nüfus Sayımı. Census of Population. Nüfusun Sosyal ve Ekonomik Nitelikleri. Social and Economic Characteristics of Population. Ankara.

DIRIMTEKIN, F. (no date): Saint Sophia Museum. Touring and Automobile Club of Turkey. Istanbul.

DÖKMECI, V., ALTUNBAŞ, K., YAZGI, B. (2007): Revitalization of the Main Street of a Distinguished Old Neighbourhood in Istanbul; in: European Planning Studies 15, 1. Oxford, New York, pp. 153–166.

DÖKMECI, V., BERKÖZ, L. (1994): Transformation of Istanbul from a Monocentric to a Polycentric City; in: European Planning Studies 2, 2. Oxford, New York, pp. 193–205.

DÖKMECI, V., SALTA, N. (1999): The Evolution and Distribution of Hotels in Istanbul; in: European Planning Studies 7, 1. Oxford, New York, pp. 99–109.

DUCELLIER, A. (1986) (ed.): Byzanz. Das Reich und die Stadt. Frankfurt, New York, Paris.

ECKARDT, F., WILDNER, K. (eds.) (2008): Public Istanbul. Spaces and Spheres of the Urban. Bielefeld.

ERGUN, N. (2004): Gentrification in Istanbul; in: Cities 21, 5. Oxford, pp. 391–405.

ESEN, O., RIENIETS, T. (2008): Fortress Istanbul. Gated Communities and Socio-Urban Transformation; in: ECKARDT, F., WILDNER, K. (eds.): Public Istanbul. Spaces and Spheres of the Urban. Bielefeld, pp. 83–111.

FAROQHI, S., McGOWAN, B., QUATERT, D., PAMUK, Ş. (1994): An Economic and Social History of the Ottoman Empire. Vol. 2, 1600–1914. Cambridge.

FRANK, R., ÜÇER, Y. (1988): Istanbul – Manhattan am Bosporus? In: Bauwelt 79, 40. Berlin, pp. 1226–1227.

FREY, F.W. (1964/1970): Education; in: WARD, R.E., RUSTOW, D.A. (eds.): Political Modernization in Japan and Turkey. New Jersey, pp. 205–235.

FRIEDMANN, J. (1986): The World City Hypothesis; in: Development and Change 17. London, Beverly Hills, Delhi, pp. 69–83.

GENIŞ, S. (2007): Producing Elite Localities. The Rise of Gated Communities in Istanbul; in: Urban Studies 44, 4. Oxford, New York, pp. 771–798.

GERHARD, U. (2004): Global Cities – Anmerkungen zu einem aktuellen Forschungsfeld; in: Geographische Rundschau 56. Braunschweig, pp. 4–10.

GOODWIN, G. (1971): A History of Ottoman Architecture. Baltimore.

GORYS, A. (2003): Istanbul. Köln.

GROTHUSEN, K.-D. (1985) (ed.): Türkei. Südosteuropa-Handbuch IV. Göttingen.

GÜLERSOY, G. (1989): Tramvay Istanbul' da. Istanbul.

GÜRSEL, Y. (1988): Big Business in Istanbul; in: Bauwelt 79, 40. Berlin, pp. 1734–1735.

GÜVENÇ, M. (2008): Mapping Social Istanbul. Extracts of the Istanbul Metropolitan Area Atlas; in: ECKARDT, F., WILDNER, K. (eds.): Public Istanbul. Spaces and Spheres of the Urban. Bielefeld, pp. 21–27.

GÜVENÇ, M., IŞIK, O. (2202): A Metropolis at the Crossroads: The Changing Social Geography under the Impact of Globalization; in: MARCUSE, P., VAN KEMPEN, R. (eds.): Of States and Cities. The Partitioning of Urban Space. Oxford, pp. 200–217.

HALL, P. (1966): The World Cities. London.

HALL, P. (1966): Weltstädte. München.

HALL, Sir P. (2001/2008): Global City-Region. Trends, Theory, Policy; in: SCOTT, A.J. (ed.): Global City-Regions in the Twenty-first Century. Oxford, pp. 59–77.

HANNERZ, U. (1992): Cultural Complexity. Studies in the Social Organization of Meaning. New York.

HANNERZ, U. (2006): The Cultural Role of World Cities; in: BRENNER, N., KEIL, R. (eds.): The Global Cities Reader. London, New York, pp. 313–318.

HANSON, H. (1967): Konstantinopels Kirchen und die Moscheen Istanbuls; in: BECHTELER, K. (ed.): Istanbul. Beiträge zur Geschichte und Entwicklung der Stadt am Goldenen Horn. Ludwigsburg, pp. 89–129 (part 1), pp. 191–266 (part 2).

HAUSSIG, H.-W. (1959): Kulturgeschichte von Byzanz. Stuttgart.

HEARSEY, J.E.N. (1963): City of Constantine 324–1453. London.

HELLER, W., GERDES, D. (1991): Stadtumbau in Istanbul. Zur Verlegung von Betrieben des Großhandels, des Handwerks und der Industrie vom "Goldenen Horn" seit 1980. Ein Beitrag zur Angewandten Stadtgeographie; in: Zeitschrift für Wirtschaftsgeographie 35. Frankfurt am Main, pp. 24–36.

HOFMEISTER, B. (1969): Stadtgeographie. Braunschweig (Series: Das Geographische Seminar).

HÖGG, H. (1967): Istanbul, Stadtorganismus und Stadterneuerung; in: BECHTELER, K. (ed.): Istanbul. Beiträge zur Geschichte und Entwicklung der Stadt am Goldenen Horn. Ludwigsburg, pp. 281–349.

HÜBNER, K., KAMLAH, P., REINFANDT, L. (eds.) (2001): Die Seidenstraße. Handel und Kulturaustausch in einem eurasiatischen Wegenetz. Asien und Afrika. Beiträge des Zentrum für Asiatische und Afrikanische Studien (ZAAS) der Christian-Albrechts-Universität zu Kiel 3. 2nd ed. Schenefeld.

INALCIK, h. (1973): The Ottoman Empire. The Classical Age 1300–1600. London.

ISIN, E.F. (2001): Islamization and Globalization; in: SCOTT, A.J. (ed.): Global City-Regions. Trends, Theory, Policy. Oxford, pp. 349–368.

JANIN, R. (1964): Constantinople Byzantine. Paris (Institut Français d'Études Byzantines).

JANSEN, U. (2004): Metropolstadt Istanbul im Wandel; in: Praxis Geographie 34. Braunschweig, pp. 44–47.

JASTROW, J. (1915): Die Weltstellung Konstantinopels in ihrer historischen Entwicklung. Weimar (Series: Deutsche Orient-Bücherei 4).

JIREČEK, C.J. (1877): Die Heerstraße von Belgrad nach Constantinopel und die Balkanpässe. Eine historisch-geographische Studie. Prag.

KARPAT, K. (1976): The Gecekondu: Rural Migration and Urbanization. Cambridge.

KEYDER, Ç. (ed.) (1999): Istanbul. Between the Global and the Local. Lanham, Boulder, New York, Oxford.

KEYDER, Ç. (1999): The Housing Market from Informal to Global; in: KEYDER, Ç. (ed.): Istanbul. Between the Global and the Local. Lanham, Boulder, New York, Oxford, pp. 143–159.

KEYDER, Ç., ÖNCÜ, A. (1993): Istanbul and the Concept of World Cities. Istanbul (Series: Friedrich-Ebert-Foundation).

KING, A.D. (ed.) (1997/2007): Culture, Globalization and the World System. Contemporary Conditions for Representation of Identity. Minneapolis.

KIENITZ, F.K. (1959). Türkei: Anschluß an die moderne Wirtschaft unter Atatürk. Schriften des Hamburger Weltwirtschafts-Archivs 10. Hamburg.

KIRSTEN, E. (1956): Die griechische Polis als historisch-geographisches Problem des Mittelmeerraumes. Colloquium Geographicum 5. Bonn.

KIRSTEN, E. (1958): Die byzantinische Stadt; in: Berichte zum XI. Internationalen Byzantinisten-Kongreß, München 1958. München, pp. 1–48.

KIRSTEN, E., BUCHHOLZ, E.W., KÖLLMANN, W. (eds.) (1956): Raum und Bevölkerung in der Weltgeschichte. Bevölkerungs-Ploetz. 2 vols. 2nd ed. Würzburg.

KNOX, P.L., TAYLOR, P.J. (eds.) (1995): World Cities in a World System. Cambridge.

KOLB, F. (1984): Die Stadt im Altertum. München.

KÖMÜRCÜOĞLU, E.A. (1966): Das alttürkische Wohnhaus. Wiesbaden.

KRÄTKE, S. (2002): Medienstadt. Urbane Cluster und globale Zentren der Kulturproduktion. Opladen.

KREISER, K. (2000): Istanbul. Ein historisch-literarischer Stadtführer. München.

KÜÇÜKERMAN, Ö. (1992): Das alttürkische Wohnhaus. Auf der Suche nach der räumlichen Identität. 5th ed. Istanbul (Series: Türkischer Touring und Automobilclub).

KULOĞLU, C. (1998): Finanzplatz Istanbul; in: Stadt Bauwelt 89, 36. Berlin, pp. 2018–2021.

KÜNZLER-BEHNCKE, R. (1960): Entstehung und Entwicklung fremdvölkischer Eigenviertel im Stadtorganismus. Ein Beitrag zum Problem der "primären Viertelsbildung". Frankfurter Geographische Hefte 33/34. Frankfurt am Main.

LEHMANN, J. (1967): Die byzantinische Mosaikkunst; in: BECHTELER, K. (ed.): Istanbul. Beiträge zur Geschichte und Entwicklung der Stadt am Goldenen Horn. Ludwigsburg, pp. 81–88.

LEITNER, W. (1965): Die innerurbane Verkehrsstruktur Istanbuls; in: Mitteilungen der Österreichischen Geographischen Gesellschaft 107. Wien, pp. 45–70.

LEITNER, W. (1967): Der Hafen von Stambul; in: BECKEL, L., LECHLEITNER, H. (eds.): Festschrift für L.G. Scheidl zum 60. Geburtstag 2. Wien, pp. 93–107.

LEITNER, W. (1969): Die Standorts- bzw. Lokalisationsfaktoren der Istanbuler Industrie. Graz.

LEITNER, W. (1971): Die Industriefunktion der Halbinsel Stambul. Ein Beitrag zur Funktionsviertelstruktur der "Stadt am Goldenen Horn" – Istanbul; in: Geographischer Jahresbericht aus Österreich 33. Wien, pp. 141–156.

LEITNER, W. (1986): Zur Religionsgeographie bzw. Geisteshaltung am Beispiel Galatas, eines Istanbuler Stadtteils; in: BÜTTNER, M., HOHEISEL, K., KÖPF, U., RINSCHEDE, G., SIEVERS, A. (eds.): Religion und Siedlungsraum. Geographica Religionum 2. Berlin, pp. 179–223.

LEITNER, W. (1989): Die türkischen Metropolen Ankara und Istanbul im Vergleich. Ein Beitrag zur Zentralitätsforschung und zur Ermittlung von Großstadtregionen; in: Mitteilungen der Österreichischen Geographischen Gesellschaft 131. Wien, pp. 109–144.

LEWIS, B. (1961): The Emergence of Modern Turkey. London, New York, Toronto.

LICHTENBERGER, E. (1998): Stadtgeographie 1. Begriffe, Konzepte, Modelle, Prozesse. 3rd ed. Stuttgart, Leipzig (Series: Teubner Studienbücher Geographie).

MANTRAN, R. (1962): Istanbul dans la seconde moitié du XVIIe siècle. Essai d'histoire institutionelle, économique et sociale. Paris (Bibliothèque Archéologique et Historique de l'Institut Français d'Archéologie d'Istanbul XII).

MANTRAN, R. (ed.) (1989): Histoire de l'Empire Ottoman. Paris.

MANTRAN, R. (1996): Histoire d'Istanbul. Paris.

MARCUSE, P., VAN KEMPEN, R. (eds.) (2002): Of States and Cities. The Partitioning of Urban Space. Oxford (Series: Oxford Geographical and Environmental Studies).

MATUZ, J. (1985): Warum es in der ottomanischen Türkei keine Industrieentwicklung gab; in: Südosteuropa-Mitteilungen 24. München, pp. 43-46.

MATUZ, J. (1990): Das Osmanische Reich. Grundlinien seiner Geschichte. 2nd ed. Darmstadt.

MAYER, H.E. (1965): Geschichte der Kreuzzüge. Stuttgart (Series: Urban Bücher 86).

MAYER, R. (1943): Byzantion - Konstaninopel - Istanbul. Eine genetische Stadtgeographie. Akademie der Wissenschaften in Wien, Philosophisch-historische Klasse. Denkschriften. Vol. 71, 3. Section. Wien, Leipzig.

MERLE, H. (1916): Die Geschichte der Städte Byzantion und Kalchedon von ihrer Gründung bis zum Eingreifen der Römer in die Verhältnisse des Ostens. Kiel (Dissertation).

METZ, H.C. (ed.) (1996): Turkey, a Country Study. 3rd ed. Washington.

MEYER, TH. (1997): Identitäts-Wahn. Die Politisierung des kulturellen Unterschieds. Berlin.

MITCHELL, B.R. (1975): European Historical Statistics, 1750–1970. New York.

MOSS, M.L. (1987): Telecommunications, World Cities and Urban Policy; in: Urban Studies 24. Oxford, New York, pp. 534–546.

MÜLLER-WIENER, W. (1977): Bildlexikon zur Topographie Istanbuls. Byzantion – Konstantinupolis – Istanbul bis zum Beginn des 17. Jahrhunderts. Tübingen.

MÜLLER-WIENER, W. (1982): Die geschichtliche Entwicklung des Quartiers Zeyrek und seine Baudenkmäler; in: MÜLLER-WIENER, W., CRAMER, C. (eds.): Istanbul-Zeyrek. Studien zur Erhaltung eines traditionellen Wohngebiets. Mitteilungen des Deutschen Orient-Instituts 17. Hamburg, pp. 15–28.

MÜLLER-WIENER, W (1988): Manufakturen und Fabriken in Istanbul vom 15.–19. Jahrhundert; in: Mitteilungen der Fränkischen Geographischen Gesellschaft 33/34. Erlangen, pp. 257–320.

MÜLLER-WIENER, W. (1994): Die Häfen von Byzantion, Konstantinupolis, Istanbul. Tübingen.

NEBIOĞLU, O. (1941): Die Auswirkungen der Kapitulationen auf die türkische Wirtschaft. Probleme der Weltwirtschaft 68. Schriften des Instituts für Weltwirtschaft an der Universität Kiel. Jena.

NEWSKAJA, P. (1955): Byzanz in der klassischen und hellenistischen Epoche. Leipzig.

NICOLLE, D., HOOK, CH. (2000): Constantinople 1453. The End of Byzantium. Oxford (Series: Osprey, Campaigns).

NOLLER, P. (1999): Globalisierung, Lebensstile und Stadträume. Kulturelle und lokale Repräsentationen des globalen Raumes. Opladen.

OLBRICHT, K. (1933): Weltstädte heute und einst; in: Geographische Wissenschaft 7. Breslau, pp. 7–12.

ÖZDEMIR, D. (2002): The Distribution of Foreign Direct Investments in the Service Sector in Istanbul; in: Cities 19, 4. Oxford, pp. 249–259.

ÖZGÜÇ, N. (1986): L'Industrie en Turquie d'Après les Recensements Industriels; in: Travaux de l'Institut de Géographie de Reims 65/66. Reims, pp. 49–61.

ÖZGÜÇ, N. (1986/1987): L'Industrie en Turquie d'Après les Recensements Industriels; in: Review of the Department of Geography of the University of Istanbul 1. Istanbul, pp. 37–60.

ÖZGÜÇ, N., MITCHELL, W. (2000): Şehirlerin alternatif alışveriş mekanları: Istanbul 'da haftalık pazarlar; in: tarim + kuran I, 2. Istanbul, pp. 35–38 (Mimar Sinan Ünivertesi. Mimarlık Fakültesi Dergĕsi).

OZUS, E., DÖKMECI, V., KIROĞLU, G., EGDEMIR, G. (2007): Spatial Analysis of Residential Prices in Istanbul; in: European Planning Studies 15, 5. Oxford, New York, pp. 707–721.

ÖZYILDIRIM, S., ÖNDER, Z. (2008): Banking Activities and Local Output Growth: Does Distance from Centre Matter? In: Regional Studies 42, 2. Oxford, New York, pp. 229–244.

PADEL, W. (1921): Der Vertrag von Sèvres. Schriften für politische Bildung. Berlin.

PALENCSAR, F., KREIS, I. (2000): Der Osthandel am Bazaarrand von Istanbul; in: Klagenfurter Geographische Schriften 19. Klagenfurt, pp. 65–93.

PALENCSAR, F., STRMENIK, M. (2010): "Gated Communities" in Istanbul; in: Geographische Rundschau 62. Braunschweig, pp. 20–26.

PAMUK, O. (2003): Istanbul. Erinnerungen an eine Stadt. München.

PETERS, R. (1961): Geschichte der Türken. Stuttgart (Series: Urban-Bücher 54).

PITCHER, D.E. (1972): An Historical Geography of the Ottoman Empire from Earliest Times to the End of the Sixteenth Century. London.

PREHL, S. (2008): Whose Space? Whose Culture? Struggle for Cultural Representation in "French Street" of Istanbul; in: ECKARDT, F., WILDNER, K. (eds.): Public Istanbul. Spaces and Spheres of the Urban. Bielefeld, pp. 299–318.

RAMSAY, W.M. (1890/1962): The Historical Geography of Asia Minor. London, Amsterdam.

REBITZER, D.W. (1995): Internationale Steuerungszentralen. Die führenden Städte im System der Weltwirtschaft. Nürnberger Wirtschafts- und Sozialgeographische Arbeiten 49. Erlangen, Nürnberg.

ROTHFISCHER, B. (2007): Flughäfen der Welt. München.

RUNCIMAN, S. (1951–1954): A History of the Crusades. 3 vols. Cambridge.

RUNCIMAN, S. (1952): Byzantine Trade and Industry; in: POSTAN, M., RICH, E.E. (eds.): The Cambridge Economic History of Europe, Vol. 2. Trade and Industry in the Middle Ages. Cambridge, pp. 86–118.

RUSSELL, J.C. (1958/1961): Late Ancient and Medieval Population. Transactions of the American Philosophical Society. New Series 48, 3. Philadelphia.

RUSSELL, J.C. (1972): Medieval Regions and their Cities. Newton Abbot.

SASSEN, S. (2000): Die "Global City". Einführung in ein Konzept und seine Geschichte; in: Mitteilungen der Österreichischen Geographischen Gesellschaft 142. Wien, pp. 193–214.

SASSEN, S. (2006): Cities in a World Economy. 3rd ed. Thousand Oaks, London, New Delhi (Series: Sociology for a New Century).

SARAN, N. (1974): Squatter Settlement (Gecekondu) Problems in Istanbul; in: BENEDICT, P., TÜMERTEKIN, E., MANSUR, F. (eds.): Turkey. Geographic and Social Perspectives. London, pp. 327–361.

SCHÄFER, H. (1978): Byzantinische Architektur. München (Series: Heyne Stilkunde).

SCHARABI, M. (1985): Der Bazar. Das traditionelle Wirtschaftszentrum im Nahen Osten und seine Handelseinrichtungen. Tübingen.

SCHNEIDER, A.M. (1949): Die Bevölkerung Konstantinopels im 15. Jahrhundert; in: Nachrichten der Akademie der Wissenschaften in Göttingen, Philosophisch-historische Klasse 9. Göttingen, pp. 233–244.

SCHNEIDER, A.M. (1950): Regionen und Quartiere in Istanbul; in: Istanbuler Forschungen 17. Kleinasien und Byzanz. Gesammelte Aufsätze zur Altertums- und Kunstgeschichte. Berlin, pp. 149–158.

SCHNEIDER, A.M. (1956): Konstantinopel. Gesicht und Gestalt einer Weltmetropole. Mainz, Berlin.

SCHUBERT, A. (1996): Politische Ökonomie der Handelsliberalisierung in der Türkei 1980–1990. Gotha (Series: Nahost und Nordafrika. Studien zu Politik und Wirtschaft, Neuerer Geschichte, Geographie und Gesellschaft).

SCHULTZE, J.H. (ed.) (1959): Zum Problem der Weltstadt. Berlin.

SCOTT, A.J. (1997): The Cultural Economy of Cities; in: International Journal of Urban and Regional Studies 21. Oxford, Boston, pp. 323–339.

SCOTT, A.J. (ed.) (2001): Global City-Regions. Trends, Theory, Policy. Oxford.

SHAW, S.J. (1976): History of the Ottoman Empire and Modern Turkey. Vol. I. Empire of the Gazis. The Rise and Decline of the Ottoman Empire 1280–1808. Cambridge.

SHAW, S.J., SHAW, E.K. (1977): History of the Ottoman Empire and Modern Turkey. Vol. II. Reform, Revolution and Republic. The Rise of Modern Turkey 1808–1975. Cambridge.

SEGER, M. (1999): Istanbul – Primate City zwischen den Welten; in: Geographische Rundschau 51. Braunschweig, pp. 562–569.

SEGER, M., PALENCSAR, F. (2003): Istanbul – der Weg zurück zur Weltstadt; in: Petermanns Geographische Mitteilungen 147. Gotha, pp. 74–83.

SEGER, M., PALENCSAR, F. (2006): Istanbul. Metropole zwischen den Kontinenten. Berlin, Stuttgart (Series: Urbanization of the Earth).

SEGER, M. (2010): Stadtentwicklung und Segregation im Großraum Istanbul; in: Geographische Rundschau 62. Braunschweig, pp. 562–569.

ŞEN, F., AKKAYA, Ç., ÖZBEK, Y. (1998): Länderbericht Türkei. Darmstadt.

SMITH, M.P., FENGIN, J.R. (eds.) (1987): The Capitalist City. Oxford, New York.

SOMER, (ed.) (2005): Istanbul Kulanma Kılavuzu. Istanbul Büyükşehir Belediyesi. Istanbul.

SUMNER-BOYD, M., FREELY, J.C. (1972): Strolling through Istanbul. A Guide to the City. Istanbul.

SÖNMEZ, M. (1994): Grafiklerle 1990' larda Istanbul. Statistical Guide to Istanbul in the 1990s. Istanbul.

SOUSA, N. (1935): The Capitulary Regime of Turkey. Its History, Origin, Nature. Baltimore.

STANDL, H. (1994): Der Industrieraum Istanbul. Genese der Standortstrukturen und aktuelle Standortprobleme des verarbeitenden Gewerbes in der türkischen Wirtschaftsmetropole. Bamberger Geographische Schriften 14. Bamberg.

STEINECKE, A. (2007): Kulturtourismus. Marktstrukturen, Fallstudien, Perspektiven. München, Wien.

STEWIG, R. (1964): Byzanz – Konstantinopel – Istanbul. Ein Beitrag zum Weltstadtproblem. Schriften des Geographischen Instituts der Universität Kiel XXII, 2. Kiel.

STEWIG, R. (1964): Der Grundriß von Stambul. Vom orientalisch-osmanischen zum europäisch-kosmopolitischen Grundriß; in: SANDNER, G. (ed.): Kulturraumprobleme in Ostmitteleuropa und Asien; Schriften des Geographischen Instituts der Universität Kiel XXIII. Kiel, pp. 195–225.

STEWIG, R. (1965): The Development of Road Communications between Central Europe and the Orient via Beograd, Sofiya, Istanbul; in: Geografia 4, 1, 2. Karachi, pp. 1–10.

STEWIG, R. (1966): Bemerkungen zur Entstehung des orientalischen Sackgassengrundrisses am Beispiel der Stadt Istanbul; in: Mitteilungen der Österreichischen Geographischen Gesellschaft 108. Wien, pp. 26–47.

STEWIG, R. (1966): Ankara. Standortaspekte einer Hauptstadtverlagerung; in: Zeitschrift für Wirtschaftsgeographie 10. Hagen, pp. 180–185.

STEWIG, R. (1969): Izmit, Nordwestanatolien; in: Geographische Zeitschrift 57. Wiesbaden, pp. 268–285.

STEWIG, R. (1972): Die Industrialisierung in der Türkei; in: Die Erde 103. Berlin, pp. 24–47.

STEWIG, R. (1977): Der Orient als Geosystem. Schriften des Deutschen Orient-Instituts Hamburg. Opladen.

STEWIG, R. (1983): Die Stadt in Industrie- und Entwicklungsländern. Universitätstaschenbuch 1247. Paderborn, München, Wien, Zürich.

STEWIG, R. (1986): The Conditions of Endogenous Tourism in the Istanbul Area; in: Turing. Türkiye Turing ve Otomobil Kurumu Belleteni. Sayı 74/353. Istanbul, pp. 64–66.

STEWIG, R. (1986): Einige Beobachtungen über arabischen Tourismus in Europa; in: Orient 27. Opladen, pp. 165–167.

STEWIG, R. (1998): Wandlungen einer byzantinischen Zysterne in der Altstadt von Istanbul; in: Materialia Turcica 19; Göttingen, pp. 69–76.

STEWIG, R. (1998): Entstehung der Industriegesellschaft in der Türkei. Part I: Entwicklung bis 1950. Kieler Geographische Schriften 96. Kiel.

STEWIG, R. (1999): Entstehung der Industriegesellschaft in der Türkei. Part II: Entwicklung 1950–1980. Kieler Geographische Schriften 99. Kiel.

STEWIG, R. (2000): Entstehung der Industriegesellschaft in der Türkei. Part III: Entwicklung seit 1980. Kieler Geographische Schriften 102. Kiel.

STEWIG, R. (2000): An Attempt at Evaluation of Turkey's Position in the Old World; in: BALLAND, D. (ed.): Hommes et Terres d'Islam. Mélange Offert a Xavier de Planhol, 2 vols. Bibliothèque Iranienne 63, vol. 2. Teheran, pp. 309–321.

STEWIG, R. (2004): Die Türkei auf dem Weg von der Agrar- zur Industriegesellschaft; in: Orient 45. Wiesbaden, pp. 125–140.

STEWIG, R. (2006): Entwicklung der innerstädtischen Verkehrserschließung Istanbuls im Spiegel gesellschaftlicher Transformation in der Türkei; in: GANZ, P., PRIEBS, A., WEHRHAHN, R. (eds.): Kulturgeographie der Stadt. Festschrift für J. Bähr. Kieler Geographische Schriften 111. Kiel, pp. 605–633.

STEWIG, R. (2006): Traffic Functions of the Bosphorus; in: Orient 47. Baden-Baden, pp. 97–118.

STEWIG, R. (2006): Proposal for Including the Bosphorus, a Singularly Integrated Natural, Cultural and Historical Sea- and Landscape, in the UNESCO World Heritage Inventory. Kieler Geographische Schriften 113. Kiel.

STEWIG, R. (2006): Istanbul: literarisch; Istanbul: wissenschaftlich – zwei umfangreiche, neue Darstellungen der Stadt; in: Orient 47. Baden-Baden, pp. 609–619.

STEWIG, R. (2006): Bizans Sanarcı'dan Rekreasyon Alamina: Istanbul'un Eski Bir Semtinde Arasi Kullanışındaki Değişimler; in: ÖZGÜÇ, N., TIMOR, A.N. (eds.): Insan ve Mekân. Prof. Dr. Erol Tümertekin'e 80. Yıl Armaganı. Istanbul, pp. 99–104. (Translation: N. ÖZGÜÇ).

STEWIG, R. (2009): From Bazaar to Shopping-Center in Istanbul. Asien und Afrika. Beiträge des Zentrums für Asiatische und Afrikanische Studien (ZAAS) der Christian-Albrechts-Universität zu Kiel 13. Kiel.

STOKES, M. (1999): Sounding Out. The Culture Industry and the Globalization of Istanbul; in: KEYDER, Ç. (ed.): Istanbul. Between the Global and the Local. Lanham, Boulder, New York, Oxford, pp. 121–139.

STREN, R. (2001/2008): Local Governance and Social Diversity in the Developing World: New Challenges for Globalizing City-Regions; in: SCOTT, A.J. (ed.): Global City-Region. Trends, Theory, Policy. Oxford, pp. 193–213.

SUZUKI, P. (1966): Peasants without Plows: some Anatolians in Istanbul; in: Rural Sociology 31. Madison, pp. 428–438.

TAESCHNER, F. (1924/1926): Das anatolische Wegenetz nach osmanischen Quellen. Türkische Bibliothek XXII, Leipzig 1924. XXIII, Leipzig 1926.

TAESCHNER, F. (1926): Die Verkehrslage und das Wegenetz Anatoliens im Wandel der Zeiten; in: Petermanns Geographische Mitteilungen 72. Gotha, pp. 202–206.

TIMBERLAKE, M. (ed.) (1985/2009): Urbanization in the World-Economy. Orlando, San Diego, New York, London, Toronto, Montreal, Sydney, Tokyo.

TIMOR, A.N. (2004): Yagınlaşan Bir Pazarlama Yöntemi: Modern Alışveriş Merkezleri ve Türkiye'deki Durumu. Istanbul.

TOKATLI, N., BOYACI, Y. (1998): The Changing Retail Industry and Retail Landscapes. The Case of post-1980 Turkey; in: Cities 15,5. Oxford, pp. 345–357.

TOKATLI, N., BOYACI, Y. (1999): The Changing Morphology of Commercial Activity in Istanbul; in: Cities 16,3. Oxford, pp. 181–193.

TÜMERTEKIN, E. (1961): L'Activité Industrielle à Istanbul; in: Review of the Geographical Institute of the University of Istanbul. International Edition 7. Istanbul, pp. 35–52.

TÜMERTEKIN, E. (1971): Manufacturing and Suburbanization in Istanbul; in: Review of the Geographical Institute of the University of Istanbul. International Edition 13. Istanbul, pp. 1–40.

TÜMERTEKIN, E. (1972): Analysis of the Location of Industry in Istanbul. Publication of Istanbul University 1808. Publication of Geographical Institute 71. Istanbul.

TÜMERTEKIN, E. (1979): Istanbul 'da Nüfus Dağılışı. La Distribution de la Population en Istanbul. Istanbul Üniversitesi Yayin 2540. Publication de l'Université d'Istanbul 2540. Coğrafya Enstitüsü Yayın 104. Publication de l'Institut de Géogaphie 104. Istanbul.

TÜMERTEKIN, E., ÖZGÜÇ, N. (1977): Distribution of Out Born Population in Istanbul. A Case Study on Migration. Istanbul.

UZUN, C.N. (2001): Gentrification of Istanbul: A Diagnostic Study. Nederlandse Geografische Studies 285. Utrecht.

UZUN, C.N. (2003): The Impact of Urban Renewal and Gentrification on Urban Fabric: Three Cases in Turkey; in: Tijdschrift for Economische en Sociale Geografie 94, 3. Oxford, pp. 363–375.

VAN DER MEER, F., MOHRMANN, C., KRAFT, H. (1959): Bildatlas der frühchristlichen Welt. Gütersloh.

VON ROHR, G. (2008): Metropolen in Südosteuropa. Istanbul und Athen. Projektbericht und Exkursionsführer 8. Geographisches Institut. Christian-Albrechts-Universität. Kiel.

WARDENGA, U. (2005): "Kultur" und historische Perspektive in der Geographie; in: Geographische Zeitschrift 93. Stuttgart, pp. 17–32.

WELZ, G. (1996): Inszenierungen kultureller Vielfalt: Frankfurt am Main und New York. Berlin.

Welt und Umwelt der Bibel (2009): Konstantinopel. Hauptstadt des Ostens. Vol. 3. Stuttgart.

WIDEMANN, H. (1985): Hochschulen und Wissenschaft; in: GROTHUSEN, K.-D. (ed.): Türkei. Südosteuropa-Handbuch IV. Göttingen, pp. 549–566.

WIEBE, E. (1977): Raumgestaltende Wirtschafts- und Sozialsysteme in Mittelasien. Paderborn, München (Series: Fragenkreise).

WIRTH, E. (1974–1975): Zum Problem des Bazars (suq, çarşı). Versuch einer Begriffsbstimmung und Theorie des traditionellen Wirtschaftszentrums der orientalisch-islamischen Stadt; in: Der Islam. Vol. 51 (1974). Berlin, pp. 203–260. Vol. 52 (1975). Berlin, pp. 6–46.

WIRTH, E. (2001): Die orientalische Stadt im islamischen Vorderasien und Nordafrika. Städtische Bausubstanz und räumliche Ordnung, Wirtschaftsleben und soziale Organisation. 2 vols. 2nd ed. Mainz.

WOOD, A.C. (1935/1964): A History of the Levant Company. Oxford, London, Liverpool.

YERASIMOS, S. (1992)(ed.): Istanbul 1914–1923. Capitale d'un monde illusoire ou l'agonie des vieux empires. Paris (Series: Editions Autrement. Series Mémoires 14).

YERASIMOS, S. (1994): Les Turcs. Orient et Occident, Islam et Laïcité. Paris (Series: Editions Autrement. Series Monde HS 76).

YERASIMOS, S. (1997): Istanbul: naissance d'une megapole; in: Revue de Géographie de l'Est 37, 2–3. Nancy, pp. 189–215.

YERASIMOS, S. (2000): Constantinople. De Byzance à Istanbul. Paris.

YERASIMOS, S. (2000): Konstantinopel. Istanbuls historisches Erbe. Köln.

YIRMIBEŞOĞLU, F., ERGUN, N. (2003): Property and Personal Crime in Istanbul; in: European Planning Studies 15, 3. Oxford, New York, pp. 339–355.

YÜCESOY, E.Ü. (2008): Contested Public Spaces vs. Conquered Public Spaces. Gentrification and its Reflection on Urban Space in Istanbul; in: ECKARDT, F., WILDNER, K. (eds.): Public Istanbul. Spaces and Spheres of the Urban. Bielefeld, pp. 29–47.

Z/YEN GROUP (2009): The Global Financial Centres Index (GFCI) 6. (City of) London.

Weitere Titel der Reihe „Asien und Afrika"

Stephan Conermann (Hg.)
Bd. 1: Der Indische Ozean in historischer Perspektive
Der geschichtliche Hintergrund des Großraums von hellenistischer und römischer Zeit bis ins 19. Jahrhundert.
295 S., kart., ISBN 978-3-930826-44-5

Stephan Conermann (Hg.)
Bd. 2: Mythen, Geschichte(n), Identitäten
385 S., kart., ISBN 978-3-930826-52-0

Ulrich Hübner, Jens Kamlah, Lucian Reinfandt (Hg.)
Bd. 3: Die Seidenstraße
Handel und Kulturaustausch in einem eurasiatischen Wegenetz. 2. Auflage
260 S., kart., ISBN 978-3-930826-63-6

Sven Sellmer, Horst Brinkhaus (Hg.)
Bd. 4: Zeitenwenden
Historische Brüche in asiatischen und afrikanischen Gesellschaften
314 S., kart., ISBN 978-3-930826-64-3

Ulrich Haarmann
Bd. 5: Briefe aus der Wüste
Die private Korrespondenz der in Ġadāmis ansässigen Yūšaʿ – Familie
Aus dem Nachlaß herausgegeben und eingeleitet von Stephan Conermann. Arabische Privatbriefe aus dem 13. bis 19. Jahrhundert
201 S., kart., ISBN 978-3-930826-80-3

Ulrike Teuscher
Bd. 6: Königtum in Rajasthan
Legitimation im Mewar des 7. bis 15. Jahrhunderts
332 S., kart., ISBN 978-3-930826-88-9

Stephan Conermann, Anja Pistor-Hatam (Hg.)
Bd. 7: Die Mamlūken
Studien zu ihrer Geschichte und Kultur. Zum Gedenken an Ulrich Haarmann (1942-1999)
414 S., kart., ISBN 978-3-930826-81-0

Stephan Conerman, Geoffrey Haig (Hg.)
Bd. 8: Die Kurden
Studien zu ihrer Sprache, Geschichte und Kultur
275 S., kart., ISBN 978-3-930826-82-7

Ulrich Hübner, Antje Richter (Hg.)
Bd. 9: Wasser - Lebensmittel, Kulturgut, politische Waffe
Historische und zeitgenössische Probleme und Perspektiven in asiatischen und afrikanischen Gesellschaften
305 S., kart., ISBN 978-3-930826-83-4

Stephan Conermann, Jan Kusber (Hg.)
Bd. 10: Studia Eurasiatica
Festschrift für Hermann Kulke zum 65. Geburtstag
526 S., kart., ISBN 978-3-930826-99-5

Angelika C. Messner, Konrad Hirschler (Hg.)
Bd. 11: Heilige Orte in Asien und Afrika
Räume göttlicher Macht und menschlicher Verehrung
280 S., kart., ISBN 978-3-936912-19-7

Anja Pistor-Hatam, Antje Richter (Hg.)
Bd. 12: Bettler, Prostituierte, Paria
Randgruppen in asiatischen Gesellschaften
210 S., kart., ISBN 978-3-936912-53-1

Reinhard Stewig
Bd. 13: From Bazaar to Shopping Center in Istanbul
118 Seiten, kart., ISBN 978-3-86893-001-6

Titel der Reihe „Bonner Islamstudien" (BIS)

Mohammed Nekroumi
Bd. 1: Interrogation, Polarité et Argumentation
Vers une Théorie Structurale et Énonciative de la Modalité en Arabe Classique
231 S., kart., ISBN 978-3-936912-02-9

Bekim Agai
Bd. 2: Zwischen Netzwerk und Diskurs
Das Bildungsnetzwerk um Fethullah Gülen (geb. 1938): Die flexible Umsetzung modernen islamischen Gedankenguts 2. Auflage
396 S., kart., ISBN 978-3-936912-10-4

Ralf Elger
Bd. 3: Muṣṭafā al-Bakrī
Zur Selbstdarstellung eines syrischen Gelehrten, Sufis und Dichters des 18. Jahrhunderts
230 S., kart., ISBN 978-3-936912-11-1

Stephan Conermann (Hg.)
Bd. 4: Islamwissenschaft als Kulturwissenschaft I:
Historische Anthropologie
Ansätze und Möglichkeiten
385 S., kart., ISBN 978-3-936912-12-8

Nader Purnaqcheband
Bd. 5: Strategien der Kontingenzbewältigung
Der Mogulherrscher Humāyūn (r. 1530-1540 und 1555-1556) dargestellt in der „Tazkirat al-Wāqi'āt" seines Leibdieners Jauhar Āftābčī. Einschließlich einer kommentierten Übersetzung des Textes
312 S., kart., ISBN 978-3-936912-13-5

Caspar Hillebrand
Bd. 6: Evliyā' Čelebī auf der Krim
Ein Reisebericht aus den Jahren 1665 und 1666
ca. 300 S., kart., ISBN 978-3-936912-14-2

Mohammed Nekroumi, Jan Meise (Hg.)
Bd. 7: Modern Controversies in Qur'ānic Studies
226 S., kart., ISBN 978-3-936912-15-9

Stephan Conermann
Bd. 8: Die Šibāniden
Forschungsstand und Aufgaben für die Zukunft
ca. 300 S., kart., ISBN 978-3-936912-16-6

Piotr Szlanta
Bd. 9: Die deutsche Persienpolitik und die russisch-britische Rivalität 1906-1914
274 S., kart., ISBN 978-3-936912-18-0

Mehmed Öcal
Bd. 10: Die türkische Außen- und Sicherheitspolitik nach dem Ende des Ost-West-Konflikts 1990/2001
447 S., kart., ISBN 978-3-936912-21-0

Stephan Conermann/Marie-Christine Heinze (Hg.)
Bd. 11: Bonner Islamwissenschaftler stellen sich vor
383 S., kart., ISBN 978-3-936912-22-7

Heike Franke
Bd. 12: Akbar und Ǧahāngīr
Untersuchungen zur politischen und religiösen Legitimation in Text und Bild
U.a. mit zahlreichen Miniaturen in Farbe.
369 S., kart., ISBN 978-3-936912-34-0

Nejat Göyünç
Bd. 13: Das sogenannte Ǧāme'o l-Ḥesāb des 'Emad as-Sarāwī
Ein Leitfaden des staatlichen Rechnungswesens von ca. 1340. Diss. phil. Göttingen 1962. (Reprint)
ca. 350 S., kart., ISBN 978-3-86893-043-6

Otfried Weintritt
Bd. 14: Arabische Geschichtsschreibung in den arabischen Provinzen des Osmanischen Reiches (16.-18. Jahrhundert)
250 S., kart., ISBN 978-3-936912-74-6

Raja Sakrani
Bd. 15: Au croisement des cultures de droit occidentale et musulmane
Le pluralisme juridique dans le code tunisien des obligations et des contrats
321 S., kart., ISBN 978-3-936912-77-7

Tonia Schüller
Bd. 16: Mustafa Kamil (1874-1908) – Politiker, Journalist und Redner, im Dienste Ägyptens
529 S., kart., ISBN 978-3-936912-94-4

Reihe: Bonner Asienstudien (BAS)
Herausgegeben von
Stephan Conermann

Stephan Conermann, Wolfram Schaffar (Hg.)
Bd. 1: Die schwere Geburt von Staaten
Verfassungen und Rechtskulturen in modernen asiatischen Gesellschaften
Der moderne Nationalstaat in Asien, in dem Verfassungen die selbst auferlegten normensetzenden Rahmenbedingungen vorgeben.
433 S., Geb., ISBN 978-3-936912-54-8

Stephan Conermann (Hg.)
Bd. 2: Asien heute: Konflikte ohne Ende...
310 S., Geb., ISBN 978-3-936912-55-5

Stephan Conermann (Hg.)
Bd. 3: Die multikulturelle Gesellschaft in der Sackgasse? Europäische, amerikanische und asiatische Perspektiven
235 S., Geb., ISBN 978-3-936912-56-2

Stephan Conermann, Conrad Schetter (Hg.)
Bd. 4: Die Grenzen Asiens zwischen Globalisierung und staatlicher Fragmentierung
289 S., Geb., ISBN 978-3-936912-57-9

Günther Distelrath, Hans Dieter Ölschleger, Heinz Werner Wessler (Hg.)
Bd. 5: Zur Konstruktion kollektiver Identitäten in Asien
203 S., Geb., ISBN 978-3-936912-62-3

Tobias Delfs
Bd. 6: Hindu-Nationalismus und europäischer Faschismus: Vergleich, Transfer und Beziehungsgeschichte
Inkl. 1. Auflage von M. S. Golwalkar's „We or Our Nationhood Defined" 1939. Geleitwort von Hermann Kulke
229 S., Geb., ISBN 978-3-936912-63-0

Marion Frenger, Martina Müller-Wiener (Hg.)
Bd. 7: Von Gibraltar bis zum Ganges: Studien zur islamischen Kunstgeschichte in memoriam Christian Ewert
U.a. mit zahlreichen farbigen Bildtafeln
285 S., Geb., ISBN 978-3-936912-70-7

EB-Verlag Dr. Brandt | Jägerstraße 47 | 13595 Berlin

Tel.: 030 / 68977233 | Fax: 030 / 91607774
Mail: post@ebverlag.de | Internet: www.ebverlag.de

Asien und Afrika

Beiträge des
Zentrums für Asiatische und Afrikanische Studien (ZAAS)
der Christian-Albrechts-Universität zu Kiel

Band 14

Reinhard Stewig

Istanbul 2010:
European Capital of Culture?
World City | Global City | Mega City?

EB-Verlag

Das Zentrum für Asiatische und Afrikanische Studien (ZAAS) der
Christian-Albrechts-Universität zu Kiel wurde 1981 von Heribert Busse
(Orientalistik), Martin Metzger (Biblische Archäologie) und
Reinhard Stewig (Geographie) gegründet.

Die Beiträge werden herausgegeben von

Lutz Berger (Turkologie) – Horst Brinkhaus (Indologie) –
Anja Pistor-Hatam (Islamwissenschaft) –
Ulrich Hübner (Religionsgeschichte des Alten Testaments
und Biblische Archäologie) – Hermann Kulke (Asiatische Geschichte) –
Josef Wiesehöfer (Alte Geschichte)